McCall's
Company Cookbook

BY THE FOOD EDITORS OF McCALL'S

Designed by Margot L. Wolf

PUBLISHED BY ADVANCE PUBLISHERS   P.O. BOX 7200, ORLANDO, FL 32854

Contents

Acknowledgments: All photographs are by George Ratkai.

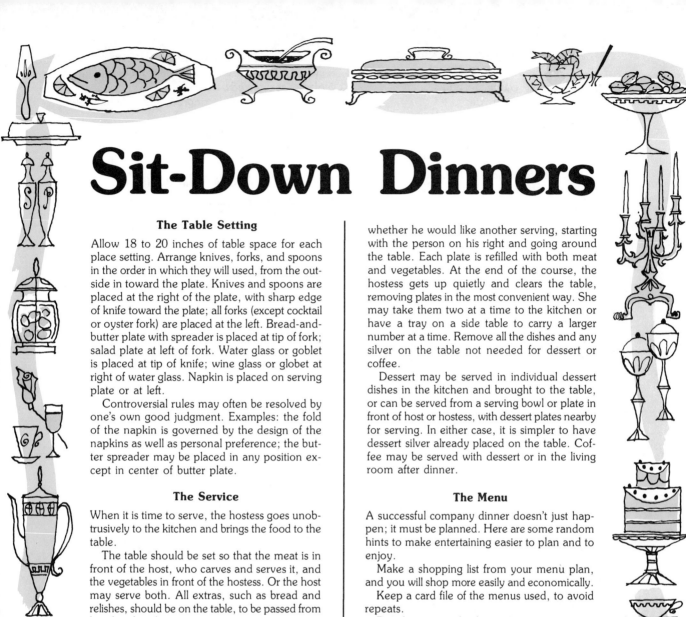

Sit-Down Dinners

The Table Setting

Allow 18 to 20 inches of table space for each place setting. Arrange knives, forks, and spoons in the order in which they will used, from the outside in toward the plate. Knives and spoons are placed at the right of the plate, with sharp edge of knife toward the plate; all forks (except cocktail or oyster fork) are placed at the left. Bread-and-butter plate with spreader is placed at tip of fork; salad plate at left of fork. Water glass or goblet is placed at tip of knife; wine glass or globet at right of water glass. Napkin is placed on serving plate or at left.

Controversial rules may often be resolved by one's own good judgment. Examples: the fold of the napkin is governed by the design of the napkins as well as personal preference; the butter spreader may be placed in any position except in center of butter plate.

The Service

When it is time to serve, the hostess goes unobtrusively to the kitchen and brings the food to the table.

The table should be set so that the meat is in front of the host, who carves and serves it, and the vegetables in front of the hostess. Or the host may serve both. All extras, such as bread and relishes, should be on the table, to be passed from hand to hand.

If one of the guests is a good friend, she might quietly get up, with no comment, and help with the last-minute preparations. When the candles are lit, announce dinner in any way that seems natural; lead guests to the table, and show them where to sit.

If there is wine with dinner, the host may open it at the table. If he opens a new bottle, he pours a little into his own glass first, to check the flavor and quality of the wine, then fills the glass of the woman on his right and so on, walking straight around the table, ending with his own glass. It is not necessary to serve all the women first.

For second helpings, the host asks each guest whether he would like another serving, starting with the person on his right and going around the table. Each plate is refilled with both meat and vegetables. At the end of the course, the hostess gets up quietly and clears the table, removing plates in the most convenient way. She may take them two at a time to the kitchen or have a tray on a side table to carry a larger number at a time. Remove all the dishes and any silver on the table not needed for dessert or coffee.

Dessert may be served in individual dessert dishes in the kitchen and brought to the table, or can be served from a serving bowl or plate in front of host or hostess, with dessert plates nearby for serving. In either case, it is simpler to have dessert silver already placed on the table. Coffee may be served with dessert or in the living room after dinner.

The Menu

A successful company dinner doesn't just happen; it must be planned. Here are some random hints to make entertaining easier to plan and to enjoy.

Make a shopping list from your menu plan, and you will shop more easily and economically.

Keep a card file of the menus used, to avoid repeats.

Develop a specialty that guests can anticipate with pleasure, but don't overdo it.

Don't repeat the same food or flavor in any one menu. Variety is the keynote to appealing dinners.

Vary the texture, flavor and color of the foods. Combine soft and crisp, tart and sweet, hot and cold. This does not mean, however, that you should serve a great many foods. The happiest menu is achieved by serving a few carefully selected, carefully prepared dishes.

Arrange foods attractively, to heighten eye appeal. A simple garnish can add a note of elegance.

(See Beauty Tips for Your Table, page 25.)

COMPANY PLANKED DINNER
Short Ribs of Beef*
with Spicy Barbecue Sauce*
Mushroom Caps
Herbed Tomato Halves*
Potato Ribbons*
Seasoned Corn*
Hot Rolls
Chocolate-Coconut Mold*
Demitasse
SERVES 4

*Recipes given for starred dishes.

SHORT RIBS OF BEEF

2½ lb short ribs of beef	¼ teaspoon dried thyme
1 teaspoon salt	leaves
¾ teaspoon pepper	2 bay leaves

1. Wipe beef with damp paper towels. Place in large saucepan with 2 cups water and all the remaining ingredients.
2. Bring to boiling. Reduce heat; simmer, covered, 30 to 45 minutes, or until beef is tender.
3. Drain; let cool. Trim fat and bone from beef; cut beef into cubes. Thread cubes on 4 skewers (5 or 6 cubes each). Arrange on planks as directed below.

SPICY BARBECUE SAUCE

8 large mushrooms	¼ cup Worcestershire
6 tablespoons lemon	sauce
juice	½ cup catsup
½ cup cider vinegar	¼ cup chili sauce
1 tablespoon light-brown	½ teaspoon dry mustard
sugar	

1. Wash mushrooms; remove stems and set aside. Toss caps with 5 tablespoons lemon juice until well coated. Make grooves in each cap, to resemble a flower. Arrange caps on planks as directed below.
2. Chop stems finely.
3. In small saucepan, combine stems with remaining lemon juice (1 tablespoon) and rest of ingredients; mix well.
4. Bring to boiling, stirring. Reduce heat; simmer, uncovered, 45 minutes, or until sauce is thick enough to coat a spoon.

HERBED TOMATO HALVES

2 medium tomatoes	2 teaspoons dried
½ cup packaged dry	oregano leaves
bread crumbs	2 teaspoons salt
2 tablespoons butter or	½ teaspoon pepper
margarine, melted	1 tablespoon chopped
	parsley

1. Cut tomatoes in half crosswise. Then make small crisscross cuts in the center of each half; arrange on planks as directed below.
2. Combine remaining ingredients in a small bowl; toss lightly with fork.
3. Before final broiling, top tomatoes with crumb mixture.

POTATO RIBBONS

2 packets (4-serving size)	½ teaspoon ground
instant mashed	nutmeg
potatoes	2 tablespoons butter or
2 teaspoons salt	margarine
¼ teaspoon pepper	

1. Prepare potatoes as package label directs, using amount of liquid specified on package, the salt, pepper, nutmeg, and butter.
2. Fill a pastry bag that has a No. 6 tip.

SEASONED CORN

2 cans (12-oz size) whole-	½ teaspoon seasoned
kernel corn, drained	salt
	¼ teaspoon pepper

Toss corn with seasoned salt and pepper.

To assemble the dinners:
1. Cover the top of each of four hardwood planks (or one large one) with foil.
2. Arrange skewer of beef cubes, 2 mushroom caps, and a tomato half on each plank. With brush, coat the beef well with some of Spicy Barbecue Sauce.
3. Place planks on rack; broil, 6 inches from heat, 5 minutes, turning beef once and brushing with sauce.
4. Remove the beef skewers, mushrooms, and tomato halves; set aside; keep warm. Remove the foil; discard.
5. Make a border around each plank by forcing Potato Ribbon through decorating tip in overlapping folds.
6. Put topping on tomato halves; arrange with beef cubes, mushroom caps, and Seasoned Corn on the planks. Brush the beef cubes with remaining sauce.
7. Broil 5 minutes, or until mushrooms are tender and potatoes golden. Add watercress.
MAKES 4 SERVINGS

CHOCOLATE-COCONUT MOLD

2 cups milk	2 eggs, separated
¼ cups sifted	½ teaspoon almond
unsweetened cocoa	extract
⅓ cup sugar	⅓ cup flaked coconut,
Dash salt	toasted
1 envelope unflavored	1 cup sweetened
gelatine	whipped cream

1. In top of double boiler, heat milk until film forms over surface.
2. Combine cocoa, sugar, salt, and gelatine in small bowl. Stir gradually into milk.
3. Place over boiling water; cook, stirring constantly, 5 minutes.
4. In small bowl, beat egg yolks slightly. Then quickly beat in a little hot cocoa mixture. Stir egg mixture quickly into remaining cocoa mixture.
5. Stirring constantly, continue to cook, over boiling water, 5 to 8 minutes, or until mixture coats a metal spoon. Cool completely.
6. Stir in almond extract and coconut.
7. In medium bowl, with rotary beater, beat egg whites until stiff peaks form.
8. Fold cocoa mixture into whites just until combined. Pour into 1-quart mold.
9. Refrigerate several hours, or until firm. Unmold; serve with sweetened whipped cream.
MAKES 6 SERVINGS

COMPANY SUNDAY DINNER

Eggs en Gelée*
Sauce Verte*
Minted Rack of Lamb*
with Fresh Asparagus* and Sautéed
Mushrooms*
Buttered New Potatoes
Spring Salad Bowl
Hot French Bread
Pineapple Savoy Trifle*
or Fresh-Strawberry Cheesecake*
Cabernet Sauvignon or Pinot Noir
Coffee   Tea
SERVES 8

*Recipes given for starred dishes.

EGGS EN GELÉE

8 eggs	¾ cup water
3 env unflavored gelatine	8 small watercress
2 cups dry white wine	sprigs
6 tablespoons tarragon	2 pitted black olives,
vinegar	sliced
3 tablespoons sugar	Watercress
¼ teaspoon salt	Sauce Verte, below

1. With a pin, prick a hole in large end of eggs. Place in medium saucepan, and cover with water to an inch above them. Bring rapidly to a boil. Take pan off heat; cover, and let stand 5 minutes. Cool under cold water to prevent further cooking.
2. Sprinkle gelatine over 1 cup water in small saucepan, to soften. Stir over low heat to dissolve gelatine. Add wine, vinegar, sugar, salt and ¾ cup water; stir until well blended.

3. Place a 1½- or 2-quart ring mold in a pan of ice and water. Pour in a thin layer of gelatine. Let stand about 5 minutes, or until gelatine is just set. Arrange 8 watercress sprigs and the olive slices in a pattern; cover with another thin layer of gelatine. Let stand until firm.
4. Meanwhile, carefully peel eggs. Place an egg on top of each olive slice and watercress sprig. Gently spoon enough gelatine around eggs to half cover them. Let stand just until set – about 30 minutes. Pour remaining gelatine over mold, and refrigerate overnight.
5. To unmold: Dip bottom of mold quickly in hot water; invert on serving plate, and shake gently to release. Garnish with watercress. Serve with Sauce Verte.
MAKES 8 SERVINGS

SAUCE VERTE

1 cup mayonnaise or cooked salad dressing	1 tablespoon chopped chives
2 tablespoons lemon juice	1 tablespoon chopped watercress
2 tablespoons chopped parsley	

1. In small bowl, combine mayonnaise, lemon juice, parsley, chives and watercress; mix well.
2. Refrigerate, covered, overnight. Serve with Eggs en Gelée.
MAKES 1¼ CUPS

As every cook knows, a bit of imagination can turn the simplest ingredients into a spectacular dish. One shining example: eggs en gelée, a delicate first course of coddled eggs, sliced olives and watercress in a shimmering gelatine ring.

At left, two Racks of Lamb (recipe page 8), surrounded by Steamed Asparagus and Sautéed Mushrooms. *Above,* a scrumptious Fresh Strawberry Cheesecake, crowned with sweetly glazed strawberries and rimmed with graham-cracker crumbs (recipe page 9).

MINTED RACK OF LAMB
(Pictured, page 7)

3½-lb rack of lamb
8 chops), 2½ lb
trimmed
1 cup fresh-bread
crumbs
1 tablespoon dried mint
leaves

1 clove garlic, crushed
¼ teaspoon pepper
2 tablespoons Dijon-
type mustard
¼ cup butter or
margarine, melted
White frills (optional)

1. Preheat oven to 375F. Wipe lamb with damp paper towels; trim off all fat. Place lamb, using rib as rack, in shallow, open roasting pan.
2. Roast, uncovered, 15 minutes for each pound of trimmed weight.
3. Remove roast from oven; let cool about 15 minutes.
4. Combine bread crumbs, mint, garlic and pepper.
5. Spread mustard over top of lamb. Pat crumb mixture into mustard, pressing firmly. Drizzle with butter. Insert meat thermometer into center of middle chop.
6. Roast 35 to 40 minutes, or until thermometer registers 160F, for medium well. Roast 5 to 10 minutes less for medium rare. Decorate with white frills, and garnish with parsley sprigs, if desired.
MAKES 4 SERVINGS
Note: For 8 servings, as pictured, use two racks of lamb and double mint mixture. If desired, use 8 rib lamb chops. Skewer chops together, to re-form rack; roast as in Step 2; apply crumb mixture to outside surface; roast to desired doneness, Step 6.

FRESH ASPARAGUS

2½ lb asparagus
Boiling water
1½ teaspoons salt
¼ cup butter, melted

Pimiento strips
Lemon wedges
(optional)

1. Break or cut off tough ends of asparagus. Wash asparagus well under cold running water. If asparagus is sandy, scrub with brush. With vegetable parer, scrape skin and scales from stalks.
2. Bunch stalks together; tie with string. Place upright in deep saucepan. Add boiling water (about 1 inch deep) and the salt.
3. Return to boiling; cook, covered, 12 to 15 minutes. Pierce lower part of stalks with fork to see if they are tender. Be sure not to overcook.
4. Drain; drizzle with butter. Garnish with pimiento strips. Serve hot, with lemon wedges.
MAKES 8 SERVINGS

SAUTÉED MUSHROOMS

1 lb fresh mushrooms
¼ cup butter or
margarine

1 tablespoon lemon juice
½ teaspoon salt
Dash pepper

1. Wash mushrooms; trim ends of stems.
2. In hot butter in medium skillet, sauté mushrooms, stirring, until tender – about 5 minutes. Add lemon juice, salt and pepper; toss lightly. Serve with Minted Rack of Lamb.
MAKES 8 SERVINGS

PINEAPPLE SAVOY TRIFLE

**Pineapple Bavarian
Cream**
3 env unflavored gelatine
3¾ cups milk
6 eggs, separated
¼ teaspoon salt
1¼ cups sugar
¼ cup dark rum

1 can (8½ oz) crushed
pineapple, drained

4 pkg (3-oz size)
miniature jelly rolls
1 cup heavy cream,
whipped

1. Sprinkle gelatine over 1 cup milk; let soften.
2. Heat remaining milk in top of double boiler, over direct heat, until tiny bubbles appear around edge.
3. In medium bowl, beat egg yolks with salt and ½ cup sugar just until well blended. Add softened gelatine. Gradually add hot milk, stirring rapidly.
4. Return mixture to top of double boiler; place over simmering water; cook, stirring constantly, until mixture coats a metal spoon – about 15 minutes. Remove from heat; cool slightly; add rum and pineapple.
5. Hasten chilling by placing pan over ice water; stir occasionally until mixture is thicker than unbeaten egg white, or until it mounds slightly when lifted with a spoon – about 30 minutes.
6. Meanwhile, line a 3-quart bowl with plastic wrap.
7. Using sharp knife, slice each jelly roll into seven (½-inch) slices. Arrange five slices in single layer to cover bottom of bowl; refrigerate. Set aside remaining slices, covered with plastic wrap, for later use.
8. In large bowl of electric mixer, beat egg whites until they form soft peaks when beater is slowly raised. Gradually beat in remaining ¾ cup sugar. Beat until stiff peaks form.
9. Add whipped cream and chilled gelatine mixture; beat at low speed just until combined – about 1 minute. Turn into prepared bowl, filling to 3 inches from top.
10. Place two rows of reserved jelly-roll slices around side of dish. Fill with remaining mixture. Refrigerate trifle until it's firm – several hours or overnight.
11. To unmold: Invert bowl on a chilled serving dish. Remove bowl; then gently peel off plastic film. Refrigerate until ready to serve. If desired, serve with more whipped cream.
MAKES 12 SERVINGS

FRESH STRAWBERRY CHEESECAKE
(Pictured, page 7)

2¼ cups packaged
  graham-cracker crums
¼ cup sugar
½ cup butter or
  margarine, softened

Filling

3 pkg (8-oz size) cream
  cheese, softened
3 tablespoons grated
  lemon peel

3 tablespoons all-
  purpose flour
4 eggs
½ cup lemon juice
1 pint box fresh
  strawberries, hulled
  and sliced

1½ cups sugar
1 pint box fresh
  strawberries
½ cup strawberry jelly,
  melted

1. Make crust: In medium bowl, with hands or back of metal spoon, mix graham-cracker crumbs with ¼ cup sugar and the butter until well combined.
2. With back of spoon, press crumb mixture to the bottom and side of a greased 10-inch springform pan.
3. Preheat oven to 350F.
4. Make Filling: In large bowl of electric mixer, at medium speed, beat cream cheese, lemon peel, sugar and flour until mixture is smooth and well combined.
5. Beat in eggs, one at a time. Beat in lemon juice. With rubber spatula, fold in sliced strawberries.
6. Pour filling into crust. Bake 40 to 45 minutes, or until center of filling seems firm when shaken.
7. Cool completely on wire rack. Refrigerate 4 hours or overnight, or until very well chilled.
8. To serve: Loosen side of pan with spatula; remove. Wash and hull 1 pint strawberries. Reserve one berry; cut rest in half. Arrange strawberries in a circle, 1 inch from edge, cut side down.
9. With remaining berries, continue overlapping inside the circle, until center is filled. Set reserved whole berry in center. Glaze strawberries with melted jelly. Refrigerate before serving.
MAKES 12 SERVINGS

Spiced Leg of Lamb*
Mixed Vegetables Italian*
Fluffy Mashed Potatoes*
Crisp Lettuce Wedges with
Thousand Island Dressing
Hot Rolls
Strawberry Parfaits*   Coffee
SERVES 6

*Recipes given for starred dishes.

SPICED LEG OF LAMB

6-lb leg of lamb
3 teaspoons salt
¼ teaspoon pepper
2 teaspoons ground
  cinnamon
2 tablespoons all-
  purpose flour

2 cups water
1 bay leaf
1 teaspoon instant
  minced onion

1. Preheat oven to 325F.
2. Wipe lamb with damp cloth; do not remove fell.
3. Combine salt, pepper, and cinnamon; rub mixture all over meat. Insert meat thermometer into fleshy part, away from bone.
4. Place on rack in shallow roasting pan. Roast, uncovered, 3 to 3½ hours, or until meat thermometer reads 160F for medium lamb, 175F for well done. Remove to heated platter; keep warm.
5. Make gravy: Pour off drippings, reserving 2 tablespoons in roasting pan. Stir in flour until smooth.
6. Gradually stir in 2 cups cold water. Then add bay leaf and onion; bring to boiling point, stirring constantly.
7. Reduce heat, and simmer 5 minutes. Serve hot, in gravy boat, along with lamb.
MAKES 6 TO 8 SERVINGS

MIXED VEGETABLES ITALIAN

1 large green pepper
  (½ lb)
3 small zucchini (¾ lb)
2 medium tomatoes
  (1 lb)
1 can (10½ oz) beef
  consommé, undiluted
½ cup water
1 teaspoons seasoned
  salt

½ teaspoon dried basil
  leaves
1 bay leaf
¼ cup butter or
  margarine
1 Bermuda onion (1 lb),
  cut into eighths
2 tablespoons chopped
  parsley

1. Wash green pepper; cut in half; remove seeds and ribs; cut into 1-inch cubes.
2. Wash unpeeled zucchini; trim ends; cut into ½-inch slices.
3. Wash tomatoes; cut into eighths.
4. In 10-inch skillet, with tight-fitting cover, bring to boiling consommé, ½ cup water, seasoned salt, basil, bay leaf, and butter.
5. Add onion; cook, covered, over high heat, 10 minutes.
6. Layer remaining vegetables on onion in following order: green pepper, zucchini, and tomatoes.
7. Cook, covered, over high heat, 5 minutes, or just until pepper is tender. Remove bay leaf.
8. With slotted utensil, arrange vegetables around lamb on serving platter; sprinkle vegetables with parsley.
MAKES 6 TO 8 SERVINGS

FLUFFY MASHED POTATOES

8 medium potatoes (about 2½ lb)
Boiling water
1 tablespoon salt
1 cup milk
¼ cup butter or margarine

1. Pare potatoes; cut in quarters. Cook in 1 inch boiling water with salt, covered, until they are tender – 20 minutes. Drain well; set aside.
2. In saucepan, heat milk and butter until butter melts – don't let milk boil.
3. Mash potatoes smoothly. Gradually beat in hot milk mixture until potatoes are smooth, light, and fluffy.
MAKES 6 TO 8 SERVINGS

STRAWBERRY PARFAITS

1 pint fresh strawberries; or 2 pkg (10-oz size) frozen, sliced strawberries, thawed
⅓ cup Kirsch
1 quart vanilla ice cream

1. Wash fresh strawberries; reserve 6 or 8 for garnish. Hull rest of strawberries; slice.
2. In shallow glass dish, toss sliced strawberries (if using frozen strawberries, do not drain) with Kirsch. Refrigerate, covered, until well chilled – at least 2 hours.
3. In 6 or 8 parfait glasses, layer strawberries with ice cream, making several layers of each, beginning and ending with berries.
4. Top each with a fresh strawberry (if using frozen strawberries, top with whipped cream, if desired).
5. Serve at once or store in freezer.
MAKES 6 OR 8 SERVINGS

A SPECIAL DINNER FOR SPRING
Hot Clam Bisque*
Roast Ham
with Pineapple-Apricot Stuffing*
Spring Vegetables*
Steamed Romaine
with Lemon Butter*
Hot Cornbread Squares
Rhubarb Meringue Pie*
Chilled Rose or White Wine
Coffee   Tea
SERVES 8

*Recipes given for starred dishes.

HOT CLAM BISQUE

2 tablespoons salad oil
¼ cup butter or margarine
1 cup coarsely chopped carrot
1 cup coarsely chopped celery
1 cup coarsely chopped leek (white part)
¼ cup all-purpose flour
½ teaspoon salt
⅛ teaspoon pepper
Dash ground red pepper
2 bottles (8-oz size) clam juice
2 cans (6½-oz size) chopped clams
½ cup half-and-half

1. In hot oil and butter in 5-quart Dutch oven or kettle, sauté carrot, celery and leek, stirring occasionally, about 5 minutes.
2. Remove from heat; add flour, salt, both the peppers, stirring until smooth. Gradually add clam juice.
3. Return to heat. Bring to boiling; reduce heat, and simmer, covered, 30 minutes.
4. Add chopped clams and half-and-half. Serve hot.
MAKES 8 CUPS, 8 SERVINGS

ROAST HAM WITH PINEAPPLE-APRICOT STUFFING

10-to 12-lb fully cooked whole ham (see Note)
1½ cups coarsely chopped dried apricots
1 cup finely chopped walnuts
1 can (8½ oz) crushed pineapple, drained
¼ cup grated fresh-bread crumbs
1 egg
½ teaspoon dried thyme leaves
1½ cups white wine
¼ cup honey
Glazed Pineapple and Apricots, page 11

1. Have butcher bone ham to make cavity for stuffing. Also ask to have about ½ pound lean ham removed from cavity and ground (or reserve and put it through the food processor) – you'll need 1 cup ground ham.
2. Preheat oven to 325F. Wipe ham with damp paper towels.
3. In large bowl, combine ground ham with dried apricots, walnuts, pineapple, bread crumbs, egg and thyme; mix well. Spoon into cavity in ham; draw opening together with poultry pins; tie with twine. Place ham, fat side up, in shallow, open roasting pan.
4. Insert meat thermometer in thickest part of meat. Pour white wine into bottom of roasting pan; cover pan tightly with foil.
5. Bake 1½ hours. Remove ham from oven; remove foil. Spread half of honey over ham.
6. Bake, uncovered, 30 minutes. Brush with remaining honey; bake 30 minutes, or until ham is golden-brown and glazed and meat thermometer

registers 130F. Meanwhile, make Glazed Pine-apple and Apricots.

7. Remove from oven. Let stand 20 minutes before removing to warm platter. Garnish with Glazed Pineapple and Apricots.

MAKES ABOUT 20 SERVINGS

Note: Or, if desired, use ½ ham; reduce baking time ½ hour. Glaze; bake to 130F on meat thermometer.

GLAZED PINEAPPLE AND APRICOTS

1 can (1 lb, 4 oz) sliced pineapple	½ cup sugar
¼ cup butter or margarine	¼ cup light corn syrup
	12 dried apricots

1. Drain pineapple, reserve liquid. In large skillet, melt butter; add sugar, corn syrup and ¾ cup reserved pineapple liquid. Bring to boiling, stirring until sugar is dissolved; simmer, uncovered, 5 minutes.

2. Place pineapple rings in syrup. Cook, uncovered, 3 to 4 minutes on each side, or just until glazed. Remove from syrup to shallow pan.

3. Add dried apricots; simmer, covered, 10 minutes, or just until tender. Return pineapple rings to apricots in syrup. Remove from heat; let stand, covered, 10 minutes.

MAKES 20 SERVINGS

SPRING VEGETABLES

12 small new potatoes (halved, if necessary)	2 teaspoons sugar
6 large lettuce leaves	1 teaspoon salt,
12 small white onions, peeled	Dash pepper
	¼ cup butter or margarine
1 lb very small carrots, pared	2 pkg (10-oz size) frozen tiny peas
2 parsley sprigs	3 to 4 tablespoons butter or margarine, melted
½ cup boiling water	

1. Scrub potatoes. Pare a strip of skin about ½-inch wide around center of each potato.

2. Line a large, heavy skillet with tight-fitting cover with four large lettuce leaves.

3. Add potatoes, onions, carrots, parsley and boiling water. Sprinkle with sugar, salt and pepper. Dot with ¼ cup butter; top with remaining lettuce leaves. Cook over medium heat, tightly covered, 15 minutes.

4. Add peas; separate with a fork. Cook, covered, 10 to 15 minutes, or until all vegetables are tender.

5. To serve, remove lettuce; drain. Turn into a warm serving dish. If desired, garnish with lettuce leaves. Pour melted butter over all.

MAKES 8 SERVINGS

STEAMED ROMAINE WITH LEMON BUTTER

2 heads (1-lb size) romaine	1 tablespoon lemon juice
1 teaspoon salt	1 lemon, thinly sliced
¼ cup butter or margarine, melted	

1. In large steamer, bring water to boiling.

2. Wash romaine carefully; sprinkle outside and inner leaves with salt.

3. Place both heads in steamer, above the boiling water. Cover; steam 15 to 20 minutes, or until just tender.

4. Drain well; place on serving platter; brush with melted butter and lemon juice. Garnish with lemon slices.

MAKES 8 SERVINGS

RHUBARB MERINGUE PIE

Rhubarb Filling

4 cups unpared rhubarb, cut into 1-inch lengths, or 1 pkg (20 oz) frozen cut rhubarb with no sugar	2 tablespoons butter or margarine
	9-inch baked pie shell
1 cup sugar	**Meringue**
3 tablespoons cornstarch	4 eggs whites (at room temperature)
⅛ teaspoon salt	¼ teaspoon cream of tartar
	½ cup sugar

1. Make Rhubarb Filling: Place rhubarb in medium saucepan.

2. In small bowl, combine 1 cup sugar, the cornstarch and salt; stir into rhubarb in saucepan. Bring to boiling, stirring.

3. Reduce heat, and simmer 5 minutes, or until mixture is thickened. Stir in butter. Pour into pie shell.

4. Preheat oven to 400F.

5. Make Meringue: In medium bowl, with mixer at medium speed, beat egg whites with cream of tartar until frothy.

6. Gradually beat in sugar, 2 tablespoons at a time, beating after each addition. Then beat at high speed until stiff peaks form when beater is slowly raised.

7. Spread over rhubarb filling, carefully sealing to edge of the crust and swirling decoratively.

8. Bake 7 to 9 minutes, or until the meringue is golden-brown. Let pie cool completely on wire rack.

MAKES 8 SERVINGS

Maple-Glazed Baked Ham*
Buttered New Potatoes*
Fresh Asparagus
with Sauce Polonaise*
Endive and Chicory Salad
Orange-Pineapple Sherbet*
Assorted Cookies
Coffee
SERVES 12

*Recipes given for starred dishes.

MAPLE-GLAZED BAKED HAM

8- to 10-lb fully cooked
  boneless ham
Whole cloves
¾ cup light-brown sugar,
  firmly packed

1 cup dark corn syrup
2 tablespoons prepared
  mustard
1 tablespoon maple
  flavoring

1. Preheat oven to 325F.
2. Place ham, fat side up, on rack in shallow, open roasting pan. Insert meat thermometer in center. Bake, uncovered, 2½ to 3 hours, or until internal temperature is 130F. Remove from oven.
3. To glaze: Turn oven temperature to 450F. Take out meat thermometer; carefully remove rind from ham.
4. With tip of knife, cut fat into diamond pattern; do not cut into ham. Insert a clove in each diamond.
5. In bowl, mix rest of ingredients. Spread half of glaze over ham, and bake 10 minutes.
6. Put on rest of glaze; bake 10 minutes.
7. For easy slicing, let ham stand 20 minutes.
MAKES ABOUT 20 SERVINGS

BUTTERED NEW POTATOES

2 lb small new potatoes,
  pared
Boiling water

4 tablespoons butter or
  margarine, melted
1 teaspoon paprika
½ teaspoon salt

1. Cook potatoes in 1 inch boiling water in large saucepan, covered, 10 minutes. Drain.
2. Turn potatoes into shallow baking pan. Brush well with 4 tablespoons butter; sprinkle all over with paprika and salt.
3. Broil, 6 inches below heat, turning frequently, 10 to 15 minutes, or until fork-tender. Potatoes should have a golden outer crust.
MAKES 6 TO 8 SERVINGS
Note: For 12 servings, double recipe.

FRESH ASPARAGUS

2 to 2½ lb asparagus
Boiling water
1½ teaspoons salt

¼ cup butter or
  margarine, melted

1. Break or cut off tough ends of asparagus stalks. Wash asparagus tips well with cold water; if necessary, use a brush to remove grit. With a vegetable parer, scrape skin and scales from lower part of stalk only.
2. Stand stalks upright in bottom of double boiler; form into a bunch, tying with string. Add boiling water to depth of 2 inches, and the salt.
3. Bring to boiling; cook, covered, 15 to 20 minutes, or just until tender. Do not overcook.
4. Drain asparagus well. Pour melted butter over it. Serve hot with Sauce Polonaise, below.
MAKES 4 TO 6 SERVINGS
Note: For 12 servings, double recipe.

SAUCE POLONAISE

6 tablespoons butter or
  margarine
¼ cup packaged dry
  bread crumbs

1 hard-cooked egg,
  sieved
2 tablespoons chopped
  parsley

1. Melt butter in small skillet. Add crumbs, and sauté 2 or 3 minutes. Pour over hot asparagus.
2. Sprinkle with egg and parsley.
MAKES 6 SERVINGS
Note: For 12 servings, double recipe.

ORANGE-PINEAPPLE SHERBET

1 env unflavored gelatine
2 cups milk
½ teaspoon salt
1 cup sugar
2 cups half-and-half
1 can (6 oz) thawed
  frozen orange juice,
  undiluted

1 can (1 lb, 4 oz)
  crushed pineapple,
  drained
12 fresh or canned
  pineapple slices,
  drained

1. Sprinkle gelatine over ½ cup milk in top of double boiler, to soften. Place over boiling water, stirring until gelatine dissolves.
2. In medium bowl, combine rest of milk with the salt, sugar, half-and-half, and orange juice. Stir in gelatine mixture.
3. Pour into 2 ice-cube trays; freeze 1½ to 2 hours, or until frozen 1 inch in from edge.
4. Turn partially frozen mixture into large bowl of electric mixer; at medium speed, beat until smooth but not melted. Stir in crushed pineapple.
5. Pour back into trays; freeze 2 hours, or until firm enough to scoop out.

6. With ice-cream scoop, quickly make 12 sherbet balls. Store in freezer until ready to serve. (Freezer-wrap if storing for several hours.)
7. To serve: Let sherbet balls stand at room temperature 10 to 15 minutes.
8. Arrange pineapple slices on serving plates. To make eating easier, cut slices into bite-size sections, but keep original shape. Place a sherbet ball on each. Garnish with mint sprig or lime curl, if desired.
MAKES 12 SERVINGS

Glazed Boiled Beef Brisket*
Horseradish Sauce*
Parsley-Buttered Boiled Potatoes
Hot Buttered Carrots
Marinated Vegetable Salad*
Crispy Herb Bread*
Mocha Ice Cream Roll*
Coffee
SERVES 6

*Recipes given for starred dishes.

GLAZED BOILED BEEF BRISKET

4-lb brisket of beef	**Glaze**
2½ quarts water	⅓ cup cooking liquid
2 leeks, cut up	from meat
2 carrots, pared	1 beef bouillon cube,
2 stalks celery, coarsely	crumbled
cut	Dash pepper
12 black peppercorns	1 teaspoon cornstarch
1 bay leaf	2 teaspoons cold water
2 teaspoons salt	Parsley sprigs (optional)
1 teaspoon dried thyme	
leaves	

1. Roll beef up tightly, jelly-roll fashion; secure with twine.
2. Bring 2½ quarts water to boiling in a large kettle. To water, add beef and other ingredients; bring to boiling. Then reduce heat; simmer, covered, about 3½ hours, or until tender.
3. Remove beef from cooking liquid. Place in shallow baking pan; keep warm. Strain cooking liquid, reserving ⅓ cup.
4. Make Glaze: In small saucepan, combine reserved liquid, bouillon cube, and pepper.
5. Combine cornstarch with 2 teaspoons cold water; stir into mixture in saucepan. Bring to boiling, stirring; mixture will be thickened and translucent.
6. Brush meat with some of glaze. Run under broiler, 6 inches from heat, 2 minutes.
7. Brush with rest of glaze; broil 1 minute longer.
8. To serve: Discard twine; cut meat into slices. Garnish with parsley sprigs, if desired. Serve with Horseradish Sauce, below.
MAKES 6 SERVINGS

HORSERADISH SAUCE

½ cup fresh bread	1 bottle (4 oz) prepared
crumbs	horseradish,
1 teaspoon cornstarch	undrained
1 cup light cream	½ teaspoon salt
	Dash pepper

1. In a medium saucepan, combine bread crumbs and cornstarch. Gradually stir in cream.
2. Cook, stirring, over medium heat, until mixture comes to a boil and is thickened; boil 1 minute.
3. Remove from heat. Stir in horseradish, salt, and pepper, mixing well.
4. Reheat gently. Serve hot.
MAKES ABOUT 1½ CUPS

MARINATED VEGETABLE SALAD

2 pkg (10-oz size) frozen	¼ cup mayonnaise or
mixed vegetables	cooked salad dressing
½ cup bottled Italian-	Crisp salad greens
style salad dressing	

1. Cook vegetables as package label directs; drain. Let cool.
2. Toss vegetables with Italian dressing, coating completely. Refrigerate, covered, at least 2 hours.
3. Drain vegetables; add mayonnaise, mixing gently. Refrigerate 1 hour.
4. To serve: Arrange chilled salad on crisp greens.
MAKES 6 SERVINGS

CRISPY HERB BREAD

1 loaf unsliced white	2 teaspoons snipped
bread	fresh thyme or
1 cup butter or	rosemary leaves*
margarine, softened	½ teaspoon paprika

1. Preheat oven to 375F.
2. With serrated bread knife, completely trim crust from bread.
3. Cut loaf in half, lengthwise. Make a cut down center of each half, being careful not to cut all the way through.
4. Then make 3 cuts crosswise, being careful not to cut all the way through. Place on wire rack in shallow pan.
5. With wooden spoon, cream butter with paprika and thyme until well blended. Spread evenly over sides and top of bread.
6. Bake 15 minutes, or until crisp and golden. To serve, cut apart with scissors or knife.
MAKES 16 SMALL SERVINGS
*Or use 1 teaspoon dried thyme or rosemary leaves.

MOCHA ICE CREAM ROLL

¼ cup sifted cake flour
½ cup sifted
　unsweetened cocoa
1 teaspoon baking
　powder
¼ teaspoon salt
4 eggs
¾ cup granulated sugar
Confectioners' sugar
1½ pints soft coffee ice
　cream

Topping
1½ cups heavy cream
¼ cup confectioners'
　sugar
1 tablespoon instant
　coffee
¼ teaspoon ground
　cinnamon

1. Preheat oven to 400F. Lightly grease a 15½-by-10½-by-1-inch jelly-roll pan. Line with lightly greased waxed paper.
2. Sift flour with cocoa, baking powder, and salt; set aside.
3. In large bowl of electric mixer, at high speed, beat eggs until thick and light. Beat in granulated sugar, 2 tablespoons at a time; then beat until very thick and light.
4. At low speed, beat in flour mixture just until combined – about 1 minute.
5. Turn into pan; bake 13 to 15 minutes, or until surface springs back when gently pressed with fingertip.
6. Turn out onto dish towel that is sprinkled with confectioners' sugar. Roll up lengthwise, towel and all.
7. Let cool, seam side down, on wire rack.
8. Unroll cake, removing towel. Spread with ice cream; reroll.
9. Wrap in foil; freeze 3 hours, or until firm.
10. Meanwhile, make Topping: In medium bowl, combine cream with rest of ingredients. Refrigerate at least 2 hours.
11. Beat topping until stiff.
12. To serve: Cut roll into 10 diagonal crosswise slices. Mound Topping on each slice.
MAKES 10 SERVINGS

Chicken Curry*
on White Rice with Raisins*
Curry Condiments
(pineapple chunks, prepared chutney, chopped
cashew nuts)
Pears Arabian*
Sesame Seed Rolls, page 21
Lemon Sherbet with Raspberries*
Coconut Macaroons
Coffee　　Tea
SERVES 6

*Recipes given for starred dishes.

CHICKEN CURRY

5-lb ready-to-cook
　stewing chicken
1 onion, stuck with
　4 whole cloves
3 celery tops
1 tablespoon salt
1 bay leaf

Curry Sauce
2½ cups hot milk
3 cups packaged grated
　coconut
½ cup butter or
　margarine

2 cloves garlic, finely
　chopped
1½ cups chopped onion
¼ teaspoon ground
　ginger
1½ tablespoons curry
　powder
2 cups chicken broth
½ cup sifted all-purpose
　flour
1 teaspoon salt
1 tablespoon lemon juice
1 cup light cream

1. In 6-quart kettle, place chicken, 12 cups water, onion stuck with cloves, celery tops, salt, and bay leaf; bring to boiling.
2. Reduce heat, and simmer, covered, 2 hours, or until chicken is tender.
3. Remove chicken; let cool. Then cut off meat in large pieces.
4. Reserve 2 cups broth; strain.
5. Make Curry Sauce: Pour hot milk over coconut; let stand 45 minutes.
6. In ¼ cup hot butter, sauté garlic, onion, and ginger until onion is tender – about 5 minutes. Stir in curry powder.
7. Turn into top of double boiler. Add chicken broth and coconut mixture.
8. Simmer, covered, over hot water, 1 hour; stir occasionally.
9. Strain mixture, pressing out as much liquid as possible. Discard coconut, garlic, and onion.
10. In medium saucepan, melt rest of butter; remove from heat.
11. Stir in flour, then strained liquid until smooth; bring to boiling, stirring constantly.
12. Reduce heat, and simmer 5 minutes, or until thickened and smooth.
13. Stir in salt, lemon juice, cream, and chicken; heat gently to boiling.
14. Serve over White Rice with Raisins, below.
MAKES 6 SERVINGS
Note: Instead of stewing chicken and broth, you can use 4 cups cooked cut-up chicken and 2 cups canned chicken broth.

WHITE RICE WITH RAISINS

2 cups long-grain white
　rice
1 cup light or dark raisins

Boiling water
3 tablespoons butter or
　margarine

1. Cook rice as package label directs; drain if necessary.

2. Meanwhile, cover raisins with boiling water; let stand 10 minutes; drain.

3. With fork, stir raisins into drained cooked rice along with butter.

MAKES ABOUT 8 SERVINGS

PEARS ARABIAN

1 can (1 lb, 13 oz) pear
  halves
1/4 cup cider vinegar
1/2 cup light-brown sugar,
  firmly packed
1 (4-inch) cinnamon stick
12 whole cloves
1/4 teaspoon ground
  ginger

1. Drain pears, reserving liquid. Arrange in shallow dish.

2. In small saucepan, combine pear liquid with remaining ingredients. Bring to boiling; reduce heat; simmer, uncovered, 30 minutes.

3. Strain hot syrup over pear halves; cool; refrigerate until well chilled, basting pears several times. Delicious with curry.

MAKES 6 SERVINGS

LEMON SHERBET WITH RASPBERRIES

1 quart lemon sherbet
2 pkg (10-oz size) thawed
  frozen raspberries,
  undrained

1. Scoop sherbet into 6 sherbet dishes; top each with 1/3 cup raspberries and juice.

2. Serve at once.

MAKES 6 SERVINGS

Antipasto Salad Platter *
Neapolitan Beef *
Buttered Zucchini
Crusty Italian Bread
Prunes in Port, with Cream *
Poundcake Squares
Caffè Espresso *
SERVES 8

*Recipes given for starred dishes.

ANTIPASTO SALAD PLATTER

4 medium tomatoes,
  sliced
Bottled Italian-style
  salad dressing
Crisp lettuce leaves
1/2 lb domestic Bel Paese
  cheese, sliced
2 cans (2-oz size)
  anchovy fillets,
  drained
1 can (8 oz) pitted ripe
  olives, drained
1 bottle (4 1/2 oz)
  artichoke hearts in
  olive oil, drained

1. Sprinkle tomato slices lightly with dressing; refrigerate until well chilled – about 1 hour.

2. Then, on lettuce leaves on large platter, place tomato slices and rest of ingredients, in individual mounds. Guests serve themselves.

MAKES 8 SERVINGS

NEAPOLITAN BEEF

Sauce
1/4 cup salad oil
1/3 cup finely chopped
  onion
3 cloves garlic, crushed
1 cup pared, diced carrot
1 1/2 cups diced celery
1 1/2 lb ground chuck
1 can (6 oz) mushroom
  caps, drained
1/2 cup sherry
1 can (6 oz) tomato paste
1 can (1 lb, 3 oz) tomatoes
1 tablespoon salt
1/2 teaspoon pepper
1/2 teaspoon dried
  oregano leaves
1/2 teaspoon dried basil
  leaves

1 pkg (8 oz) small shell
  macaroni
1 pkg (10 oz) frozen
  chopped spinach
1/2 cup buttered fresh-
  bread cubes
1 cup grated sharp
  Cheddar cheese
Grated Parmesan
  cheese

1. Make Sauce: In hot oil in large skillet, sauté onion, garlic, carrot, and celery until onion is golden – about 5 minutes.

2. Add beef; cook, stirring, until red disappears.

3. Add mushrooms, sherry, tomato paste, tomatoes, salt, pepper, oregano, and basil; simmer, uncovered, 1 1/2 hours.

4. If desired, cool; cover, and refrigerate until needed.

5. About 45 minutes before serving time, preheat oven to 350F.

6. Cook macaroni and spinach according to package directions.

7. Reheat Sauce. Add well-drained macaroni and spinach.

8. Turn into 3-quart casserole. Top with bread cubes and Cheddar cheese.

9. Bake, uncovered, 30 minutes, or until bubbly and browned.

10. Serve sprinkled with Parmesan cheese.

MAKES 8 SERVINGS

PRUNES IN PORT, WITH CREAM

1½ cups port
1 pkg (16 oz) dried prunes
1 cup granulated sugar
1 cup water
2 teaspoons vanilla
  extract

1 cup heavy cream
1 tablespoon
  confectioners' sugar
¼ cup canned flaked
  coconut

1. Pour port over prunes in large bowl; refrigerate, covered, overnight.
2. Next day, combine prunes in wine with sugar and 1 cup water in a medium saucepan; bring to boiling, covered.
3. Reduce heat, and simmer 30 minutes.
4. Remove from heat; stir in 1 teaspoon vanilla.
5. Turn into serving dish; refrigerate until well chilled – about 2 hours.
6. Just before serving, whip cream just until stiff. Fold in confectioners' sugar and rest of vanilla.
7. Garnish prunes with whipped cream. Then sprinkle with flaked coconut.
MAKES 8 SERVINGS

CAFFÈ ESPRESSO

Use dark-roast Italian coffee, fine grind, with fresh, cold water in a special Caffè Espresso pot. Follow manufacturer's directions. Serve hot, in demitasse cups, with a twist of lemon peel in each, if desired.

Stuffed Crown Roast of Pork *
with Spiced Crab Apples
Baked Acorn Squash Halves *
Buttered Green Peas
Warm Herb Bread
Angel Swirl Dessert *
Coffee   Tea
SERVES 8

*Recipes given for starred dishes.

CROWN ROAST OF PORK

5-lb crown roast of pork *
1 teaspoon salt
½ teaspoon pepper
Stuffing, below

Spiced crab apples,
  drained
Parsley sprigs

1. Preheat oven to 325F. Wipe crown roast of pork with damp paper towels.
2. Place roast in shallow roasting pan. Sprinkle with salt and pepper. Protect each rib bone with foil during roasting time, to prevent overbrowning.

Insert a roast-meat thermometer into thick part of the meat, without touching any bone.
3. Fill center of roast with crushed foil to keep crown shape during roasting.
4. Roast meat, uncovered, for 2½ hours.
5. Meanwhile, make Stuffing.
6. Remove the foil from the center of the roast. Fill center with stuffing. Cover the stuffing loosely with square of foil.
7. Continue roasting pork until internal temperature is 170F on thermometer. Remove foil from each of the rib bones.
8. Place the roast on a serving board or platter. Garnish roast with crab apples and the parsley sprigs.
MAKES 6 TO 8 SERVINGS OF TWO RIBS EACH
* Have butcher "French" chops (cut meat from ends of rib bones) and cut through backbone, for easier carving.

STUFFING FOR CROWN ROAST OF PORK

6 bacon slices, in ½ inch
  pieces
½ cup chopped onion
½ cup chopped celery
3 cups fresh white-bread
  crumbs
1 teaspoon salt
¼ teaspoon pepper

¼ teaspoon dried thyme
  leaves
½ teaspoon poultry
  seasoning
1½ cups chopped pared
  apple
¼ cup butter or
  margarine

1. In skillet, cook bacon until crisp. Crumble bacon. Set aside.
2. Pour off all but 2 tablespoons bacon fat from skillet. Add onion and celery; sauté, stirring, until tender – about 5 minutes. Remove from heat.
3. Add rest of ingredients and crumbled bacon; toss lightly to combine well.
MAKES 5 CUPS

BAKED ACORN SQUASH HALVES

4 small acorn squash
¼ cup butter or
  margarine, melted
1 teaspoon seasoned
  salt

½ teaspoon dried thyme
  leaves

1. Preheat oven to 400F.
2. Scrub squash; halve squash lengthwise; scoop out seeds and stringy pulp.
3. Arrange halves, cut side down, in shallow baking pan. Add hot water to measure ½ inch.

4. Bake squash, uncovered, 30 minutes.
5. Meanwhile, combine butter, salt, and thyme.
6. Turn squash cut side up; brush with butter mixture. Add water to pan if necessary.
7. Bake, uncovered, 30 minutes longer.
MAKES 8 SERVINGS

ANGEL SWIRL DESSERT

1 pkg (15 oz) angel-food-cake mix
½ teaspoon vanilla extract
½ teaspoon almond extract
1½ squares semisweet-chocolate, melted and cooled
2 cups heavy cream
¼ cup sifted unsweetened cocoa
¼ cup sugar
¼ teaspoon salt
½ cup coarsely chopped pecans
12 pecan halves

1. Preheat oven to 375F. Make angel-food cake as package label directs, using vanilla and almond extracts.
2. Quickly fold in chocolate, just enough to give a swirled effect.
3. Turn into ungreased 9-inch tube pan; bake, on lowest shelf of oven, 35 minutes, or until surface springs back when gently pressed with fingertip.
4. Invert pan immediately, hanging tube over neck of bottle. Let cool completely – about 1 hour.
5. Meanwhile, make filling: In small bowl of electric mixer, combine cream, cocoa, sugar, and salt; refrigerate until ready to use – at least 30 minutes. At high speed, beat just until stiff.
6. Remove cake from pan. Cut crosswise into 3 layers. On cake plate, invert top layer, cut side up. Spread with about ¾ cup filling.
7. Top with middle layer; spread with ¾ cup filling. Then put final layer in place, cut side down; use rest of filling to frost top and side completely.
8. Cover side with chopped pecans; garnish top edge with pecan halves.
9. Refrigerate until serving – at least 1 hour.
MAKES 10 TO 12 SERVINGS

Chinese-Style Beef*
with Fluffy White Rice
Tossed Green Salad
Hot Rolls
Cherry Pie Supreme*
Tea
SERVES 6 TO 8

*Recipes given for starred dishes.

CHINESE-STYLE BEEF

2-lb flank steak
2 tablespoons olive or salad oil
1 clove garlic, crushed
1 teaspoon salt
Dash pepper
¼ teaspoon ground ginger
¼ cup soy sauce
½ teaspoon sugar
2 green peppers
2 tomatoes, quartered
1 can (1 lb) bean sprouts, drained
1 tablespoon cornstarch
¼ cup water

1. Slice beef, across grain, into thin strips.
2. In hot oil in large, heavy skillet, over high heat, sauté beef with garlic, salt, pepper and ginger until browned all over – 5 minutes.
3. Add soy sauce and sugar; cook, covered, 5 minutes.
4. Remove seeds and ribs from peppers. Cut peppers into 1-inch strips; add, with tomatoes and bean sprouts, to beef.
5. Bring to boiling; cook, covered and over high heat, 5 minutes.
6. Meanwhile, make a smooth paste of cornstarch and ¼ cup water. Stir into beef mixture; bring to boiling, stirring.
7. Serve at once, with rice.
MAKES 6 TO 8 SERVINGS

CHERRY PIE SUPREME

9-inch unbaked pie shell
1 can (1 lb, 5 oz) cherry-pie filling
4 pkg (3-oz size) soft cream cheese
½ cup sugar
2 eggs
½ teaspoon vanilla extract
1 cup sour cream

1. Preheat oven to 425F.
2. Prepare pie shell. Spread half of cherry-pie filling in bottom; set rest aside.
3. Bake shell 15 minutes, or just until crust is golden. Remove from oven.
4. Reduce oven temperature to 350F.
5. Meanwhile, in small bowl, with portable electric mixer, beat cheese with sugar, eggs, and vanilla until smooth.
6. Pour over hot cherry-pie filling; bake 25 minutes. (Filling will be slightly soft in center.)
7. Cool completely on wire rack.
8. To serve: Spoon sour cream around edge of pie. Fill center with remaining cherry-pie filling.
MAKES 6 TO 8 SERVINGS

BLUEBERRY PIE SUPREME: Follow above recipe, substituting 1 can (1 lb, 6 oz) blueberry-pie filling for cherry-pie filling.

Paella Valenciana*
(with Saffron Rice)
Broccoli Amandine*
Tossed Green Salad
Hot, Buttered French Bread
Café-Sherry Sundaes*
Coffee   Tea
SERVES 8

*Recipes given for starred dishes.

PAELLA VALENCIANA
(Rice with Chicken and Shellfish)

2 (2-lb size) broiler-fryers, cut up
3 teaspoons salt
1 carrot, pared and cut into slices
1 small onion, peeled
2 bay leaves
2 parsley sprigs
6 black peppercorns
3 cups water
½ cup olive oil
4 garlic cloves, peeled and slivered
1 large green pepper cut into strips (2 cups)
1 teaspoon crumbled saffron (optional)
½ teaspoon pepper
1 jar (11½ oz) whole clams
1½ cups long-grain white rice
1 can (8 oz) artichoke hearts
2 large tomatoes, coarsely chopped (3 cups)
1 lb cooked shrimp, shelled and deveined
2 tablespoons finely chopped parsley

1. Wipe chicken with damp paper towels; set aside.
2. In large saucepan, combine giblets, ½ teaspoon salt, carrot slices, onion, bay leaves, parsley, peppercorns, and 3 cups water. Bring to boiling; reduce heat, and simmer, covered, 45 minutes.
3. Meanwhile, slowly heat oil in large Dutch oven. In hot oil, slowly brown chicken all over, a few pieces at a time, removing as it browns.
4. In same hot oil, sauté garlic, green pepper, saffron, and pepper, stirring, about 5 minutes. Arrange browned chicken pieces on top. Preheat oven to 350F.
5. Drain and discard giblets and vegetables, reserving cooking liquid. Add enough liquid from clams to make 3 cups. Add to mixture in oven.
6. Bring to boiling over medium heat. Using fork, stir in rice and rest of salt, mixing well. Bring back to boiling.
7. Bake, covered, 1 hour, stirring rice every 20 minutes.
8. Meanwhile, drain clams; cut in half. Rinse artichokes in cold water; drain well; cut crosswise into ¼-inch slices. Combine clams, artichokes, tomatoes, and shrimp in large bowl. Add to chicken and rice in Dutch oven, mixing well.
9. Bake 10 minutes longer. Arrange chicken on rice and vegetables; sprinkle with parsley.
MAKES 6 TO 8 SERVINGS

BROCCOLI AMANDINE

2 pkg (10-oz size) frozen broccoli spears
½ cup butter or margarine
3 tablespoons lemon juice
½ teaspoon salt
½ cup slivered blanched almonds

1. Cook broccoli as package label directs.
2. Meanwhile, melt butter in small saucepan. Add rest of ingredients; simmer, stirring occasionally, 5 minutes.
3. Drain broccoli; arrange in serving dish; top with the sauce.
MAKES 8 SERVINGS

CAFÉ-SHERRY SUNDAES

1½ teaspoons instant coffee
¼ cup sweet sherry
1 cup light corn syrup
1 qt. vanilla ice cream

1. In small saucepan, combine coffee and sherry, stirring until coffee is dissolved.
2. Add corn syrup; bring to boiling, stirring, over medium heat.
3. Serve warm, over ice cream.
MAKES 8 SERVINGS

Roast Stuffed Veal*
with Gravy*
Cauliflower with Lemon Butter*
Baked Tomato Halves
Tossed Green Salad Bowl
Hot Rolls
Fresh Strawberry Sherbet*
Macaroons
Coffee
SERVES 8

*Recipes given for starred dishes.

ROAST STUFFED VEAL

Wild-Rice Stuffing
1 cup wild rice
¼ cup butter or margarine
1 clove garlic
¼ cup chopped onion
⅓ cup chopped celery
1 can (3 oz) sliced mushrooms, drained
½ teaspoon salt
⅛ teaspoon pepper
¼ teaspoon dried thyme leaves
½ cup sour cream
⅓ cup light raisins

5-to-6-lb boned veal shoulder*
1 clove garlic
1 teaspoon salt
¼ teaspoon pepper
½ teaspoon dried thyme leaves
6 bacon slices

1. Make Wild-Rice Stuffing: Wash and cook rice as package label directs; drain.
2. Meanwhile, in hot butter in skillet, sauté garlic until golden; discard garlic.
3. Add onion and celery; sauté until tender – about 5 minutes. Add mushrooms, salt, pepper, and thyme; remove from heat.
4. Gradually stir in sour cream. Toss mixture lightly with wild rice and raisins, to combine well.
5. Preheat oven to 325F.
6. Wipe veal with damp paper towels. Use stuffing to fill pocket almost, but not quite, full. Draw opening together with skewers, inserted at 1-inch intervals. Lace, bootlace fashion, with twine; tie ends.
7. Rub surface with cut clove of garlic. Sprinkle with salt, pepper, and thyme.
8. Place roast on rack in shallow roasting pan. Arrange bacon slices over top. Insert roast-meat thermometer in center of roast.
9. Roast, uncovered, 2½ to 3 hours or to 180F on meat thermometer.
10. Remove to serving platter. Let stand about 20 minutes before carving; keep warm. Serve with Veal Gravy, below.
MAKES 8 TO 10 SERVINGS
*Have butcher make a pocket in veal.

VEAL GRAVY

6 tablespoons drippings from veal	1½ cups milk
1½ cups water	1 teaspoon salt
6 tablespoons unsifted all-purpose flour	⅛ teaspoon pepper
	¾ teaspoon dried thyme leaves

1. Pour off drippings from roasting pan, reserving 6 tablespoons.
2. Add 1½ cups water to roasting pan; bring to boiling, stirring to loosen and dissolve brown bits in pan. Pour off, and set aside.
3. Add reserved drippings to pan. Stir in flour to make a smooth paste; over very low heat, cook, stirring, until flour is lightly browned.
4. Gradually stir in liquid from pan along with milk; bring to boiling, stirring. Reduce heat, and simmer 3 minutes, or until thickened and smooth.
5. Add seasonings; simmer, stirring, 1 minute longer. Serve with roast veal.
MAKES ABOUT 3 CUPS

CAULIFLOWER WITH LEMON BUTTER

2 heads cauliflower (1¾ - lb each)	6 tablespoons bottled capers, drained
½ cup butter or margarine, melted	2 tablespoons chopped parsley
⅔ cup lemon juice	2 tablespoons chopped chives (optional)

1. Wash cauliflower thoroughly; cut into flowerets. Cook, covered, in 1 inch lightly salted, boiling water, until tender – about 10 minutes. Drain well.
2. Meanwhile, combine butter, lemon juice, and capers.
3. Turn cauliflower into serving dish; pour lemon butter over top. Sprinkle with parsley and chives.
MAKES 8 SERVINGS

FRESH STRAWBERRY SHERBET

1 quart fresh strawberries	⅔ cup water
1 tablespoon lemon juice	2 egg whites
1½ cups sugar	¼ teaspoon salt
1 tablespoon light corn syrup	½ cup heavy cream, whipped

1. Wash; drain and hull strawberries.
2. To purée berries, press through a food mill or sieve (or blend in electric blender, covered, about ½ minute). Measure 2½ cups purée. Stir in lemon juice.
3. In medium saucepan, combine sugar, corn syrup, and ⅔ cup water. Stir, over medium heat, until sugar is dissolved. Bring to a boil, without stirring; cook to 238F on candy thermometer, or until a little of mixture in cold water forms a soft ball.
4. In large bowl, with electric mixer at high speed, beat egg whites with salt until stiff peaks form when beater is raised.
5. Slowly pour syrup, in a thin stream, over whites, beating constantly until mixture is thick and shiny.
6. Fold whipped cream into strawberry purée. Then fold into egg-white mixture until well blended.
7. Turn into 2 ice-cube trays; freeze until mushy – about 1 hour.
8. Turn into large bowl; beat until smooth. Return to ice-cube trays; freeze again until mushy – about 30 minutes.
9. Again beat mixture until smooth; refreeze until firm.
MAKES 1¼ QUARTS

Roast Chicken*
Mashed Potatoes
Asparagus with Lemon Butter*
Avocado with Salad Greens
Hot Rolls   Radish Roses and Ripe Olives
Butterscotch-Rum Sundaes*
Poundcake Fingers
Coffee   Tea
SERVES 4

*Recipes given for starred dishes.

ROAST CHICKEN

2 (2½-lb size) whole broiler-fryers	¼ cup butter or margarine, softened
1 teaspoon salt	Paprika

Stuffing	Gravy
½ cup butter or margarine	¼ cup unsifted all-purpose flour
½ cup finely chopped onion	2 cups chicken broth,* or 2 cups canned clear chicken broth
½ cup water	
2 cups packaged herb-seasoned stuffing mix	

l. Preheat oven to 325F. Remove giblets and neck from chickens; set aside to make chicken broth* for Gravy, if desired. Wash and dry chickens inside and out; rub inside with salt.
2. Make Stuffing: In hot butter in medium skillet, cook onion until tender – about 5 minutes. Add ½ cup water and the herb- seasoned stuffing, fluffing up with fork.
3. Lightly fill body cavity of each chicken with stuffing. Bring skin over neck opening; fasten to back with poultry pin. Close body cavity with pins. Pin wings to body; then tie legs together at ends, with twine.
4. Place chickens on rack, breast side down, in shallow, open roasting pan. Brush with 2 table-spoons butter. Roast, uncovered, 45 minutes.
5. Turn chickens breast side up. Brush with remaining butter; sprinkle with paprika. Roast 1¼ hours longer, or until legs move freely when twisted and fleshy part of drumstick feels soft.
6. Remove chickens to warm serving platter; remove pins and twine. Keep warm.
7. Make Gravy: To pan drippings, add flour, stirring to make a smooth mixture. Gradually add chicken broth, stirring until smooth; bring to boiling over direct heat. Reduce heat; simmer until thickened, about 2 minutes.
8. To serve chickens: With poultry shears, cut lengthwise through backbone and breastbone of each, to make 4 halves. Serve gravy hot, along with chickens.
MAKES 4 SERVINGS

*To make chicken broth:
1. In small saucepan, combine giblets (except livers) and necks, 2 teaspoons instant minced onion, ½ teaspoon salt, 2 cups cut-up celery with 4 cups water; bring to boiling.
2. Reduce heat; simmer, covered 1 hour and 45 minutes. Add livers and 2 chicken-bouillon cubes; simmer 15 minutes longer.
3. Strain broth, pressing vegetables through sieve along with broth. Measure 2 cups.

ASPARAGUS WITH LEMON BUTTER

2 lbs fresh asparagus*	¼ cup soft butter or margarine
⅓ cup water	
½ teaspoon salt	2 teaspoons lemon juice

1. Break off tough ends of asparagus stalks. Wash asparagus tips well with cold water; if necessary, use a brush to remove grit. With vegetable parer, scrape skin and scales from lower part of stalk only.
2. With sharp knife, cut stalks on the diagonal, making bias slices about 1 inch long.
3. In medium skillet, with tight-fitting cover, bring ⅓ cup water to boiling. Add asparagus and salt; cook, covered and over high heat, 5 to 8 minutes, adding more water if necessary.
4. Drain, if necessary. Add butter and lemon juice, tossing until butter is melted.
MAKES 4 SERVINGS
*Or use 2 pkg (10-oz size) frozen asparagus cuts. Cook as package label directs.

BUTTERSCOTCH-RUM SUNDAES

1 cup butterscotch sauce	1 pint vanilla ice cream
2 tablespoons light rum	12 pecan halves (optional)
2 tablespoons butter or margarine	

1. In small saucepan, combine butterscotch sauce with rum and butter.
2. Heat, stirring, over medium heat, just until butter melts.
3. Serve sauce warm, over ice cream. Garnish with pecan halves, if desired.
MAKES 4 SERVINGS

Glazed Pork Butt*
Sweet-Potato Pie*
Broccoli with Browned Butter*
Lettuce Wedges with Fresh-Tomato Dressing*
Pickled Peaches*
Sesame-Seed Rolls*
Spicy Deep-Dish Apple Pie*
Coffee   Tea
SERVES 4

*Recipes given for starred dishes.

GLAZED PORK BUTT

2¼-lb smoked boneless pork butt	1 tablespoon wine vinegar
	1 cup orange marmalade

Glaze
½ teaspoon dry mustard

1. Night before: Place pork in heavy, 3½-quart saucepan. Add water to cover; bring to boiling. Reduce heat; simmer, covered, 2 hours, or until pork is tender.
2. Remove pork. Let cool; refrigerate.
3. Next day: Preheat oven to 400F. Place pork in a 9-by-9-by-1¾-inch baking pan.
4. Make Glaze: Combine all ingredients. Spoon glaze evenly over pork.
5. Bake 25 minutes, occasionally spooning glaze in bottom of pan over pork.
6. Remove pork to heated platter; spoon over any glaze. Let stand 15 minutes. To serve, cut crosswise into ¼-inch slices.
MAKES ABOUT 8 SERVINGS
Note: Any leftover pork may be substituted for ham in sandwiches, salads, and casseroles.

SWEET POTATO PIE

1 can (1 lb) sweet potatoes	½ cup light-brown sugar, firmly packed
	½ cup cornflakes

Topping
¼ cup butter or margarine, melted

1. Preheat oven to 400F. Grease a 7- or 8-inch pie plate.
2. Drain potatoes, reserving ½ cup liquid. Mash potatoes. Gradually add reserved liquid, stirring until well combined. Turn into prepared pie plate, spreading evenly.
3. Make Topping: Toss butter, sugar, and cornflakes, to combine. Sprinkle evenly over potatoes.
4. Bake, uncovered, 20 minutes, or until topping is golden-brown and crispy.
MAKES 4 SERVINGS

BROCCOLI WITH BROWNED BUTTER

1 pkg (10 oz) frozen broccoli spears	¼ cup butter or margarine

1. Cook broccoli as package label directs. Drain.
2. Meanwhile, melt butter in small saucepan, over low heat. Heat, stirring, until deep-golden – about 1 minute. Do not burn.
3. Pour butter over broccoli in serving dish.
MAKES 4 SERVINGS

LETTUCE WEDGES
WITH FRESH-TOMATO DRESSING

Dressing

1 cup peeled, diced tomato (1 large tomato)	2 tablespoons chopped parsley
½ cup bottled Italian-style salad dressing	¼ cup mayonnaise or cooked salad dressing
2 teaspoons instant minced onion	4 Iceberg-lettuce wedges

1. Make Dressing: Combine all ingredients, mixing well. Refrigerate at least 1 hour before serving.
2. Arrange a lettuce wedge on each of 4 salad plates. Spoon over dressing.
MAKES 4 SERVINGS

PICKLED PEACHES

1 can (1 lb) cling-peach halves	1-inch cinnamon stick
About 18 whole colves	2 lemon slices
1 whole allspice	1 tablespoon vinegar

1. Drain peaches, reserving liquid. Insert 3 whole cloves into each half. Pack into pint jar.
2. In small saucepan, bring reserved liquid, allspice, cinnamon stick, lemon slices, and vinegar to boiling. Pour over peaches; cap jar.
3. Let peaches cool. Refrigerate 2 or 3 days before using.
MAKES 4 TO 6 SERVINGS

SESAME SEED ROLLS

8 brown-and-serve rolls	1 teaspoon sesame seed
¼ cup butter or margarine, melted	

1. Brush top of each roll with melted butter. Sprinkle each with ⅛ teaspoon sesame seed.
2. Bake as package label directs. Serve warm.
MAKES 8

SPICY DEEP-DISH APPLE PIE

½ pkg (10-oz size)
  piecrust mix

Filling
2 tablespoons all-
  purpose flour
½ to ⅔ cup sugar
½ teaspoon cinnamon

1 can (1 lb, 4 oz) apple
  slices, undrained
2 tablespoons lemon
  juice
2 tablespoons butter or
  margarine
Granulated sugar

1. Prepare piecrust mix as package label directs. Refrigerate, in waxed paper, until ready to roll out.
2. Preheat oven to 425F. Lightly grease a 1-quart casserole.
3. Make Filling: In medium bowl, combine flour, sugar, and cinnamon. Add apple slices and lemon juice, tossing gently to combine. Turn apple mixture into prepared casserole, mounding in center. Dot with butter.

4. Roll out pastry to an 11-inch circle; trim to a 10-inch circle.
5. Moisten edge of casserole with water. Arrange pastry over casserole; crimp edge decoratively. Make 5 gashes in center of crust for steam vents. Sprinkle lightly with a little sugar.
6. Bake 30 minutes, or until crust is golden and juices bubble through slits in crust. Serve warm with cream, if desired
MAKES 4 GENEROUS SERVINGS
Note: Reroll leftover pastry; cut into strips. Sprinkle with cinnamon-sugar. Bake at 425F about 8 minutes, or until golden.

Company Dinners
from your Freezer

Roast Beef
Stuffed Baked Potatoes*
Broccoli Spears with Sauce Polonaise, page 12
Green Salad Bowl with Almonds
Sesame Seed Rolls, page 21
Crème de Menthe Ice Cream and Pears*
Coffee   Tea
SERVES 8

* Recipes given for starred dishes.

BEEF ROASTING CHART

Cut of Beef	Defrosted	Hard-frozen
4-lb standing rib	Rare: 1½-1¾ hrs	2-2½hrs
(300 to 325F)	Medium: 1¾-2¼ hrs	2½-3 hrs
	Well: 2½-3 hrs	3-4 hrs
4-lb rolled rib	Rare: 2-2¼ hrs	2½-3 hrs
(300 to 325F)	Medium: 2¼-2½ hrs	3-3½ hrs
	Well: 2½-2¾ hrs	3½-4 hrs

STUFFED BAKED POTATOES

4 medium Idaho
  potatoes (about 2 lb)
⅓ cup butter or
  margarine
½ cup grated sharp
  Cheddar cheese

½ cup light cream
2 tablespoons snipped
  fresh chives
¾ teaspoon salt
Dash ground red pepper
Paprika

1. Preheat oven to 425F. Scrub potatoes with vegetable brush; pierce skins with fork.
2. Bake about 1 hour, or until tender.
3. Cut potatoes in half lengthwise. With spoon, scoop out inside, being careful to leave skin intact, as shell.
4. With portable electric mixer or fork, beat potato with butter, cheese, cream, chives, salt and pepper until smooth and light.
5. Spoon mixture into shells, fluffing up in center. Sprinkle with paprika.
6. Let potatoes cool completely. Freezer-wrap; label and freeze.
7. To serve: Preheat oven to 450F. Remove potatoes from freezer; discard wrapping. Bake, uncovered, 30 minutes.
MAKES 8 SERVINGS

CRÈME DE MENTHE ICE CREAM AND PEARS

2 quarts soft vanilla ice
  cream
¼ cup green crème de
  menthe

1 can (l lb, 13 oz) pear
  halves, well chilled
1 can (8 oz) chocolate
  syrup

1. Turn ice cream into a large bowl.
2. With rubber scraper, swirl crème de menthe into

soft ice cream just enough to make streaks; do not overmix. Turn ice cream into 3 or 4 ice-cube trays, and refreeze until firm – about 4 hours.

3. To serve: Arrange drained pear halves in large compote. Mound scoops of ice cream on top. Pour on syrup.

MAKES 8 SERVINGS

Chicken Pies, Country Style*
Tossed Green Salad
Freezer French Bread*
Frozen Peppermint-Ice-Cream Cake*
Coffee   Tea
SERVES 8

*Recipes given for starred dishes.

CHICKEN PIES, COUNTRY STYLE

5-lb ready-to-cook stewing chicken	2 lb fresh peas, shelled*
8 cups water	1 can (6 oz) sliced mushrooms, drained
2 celery stalks, quartered	1 cup light cream
1 medium onion, quartered	1/4 teaspoon ground nutmeg
1/2 lemon, sliced	1/4 teaspoon celery salt
2 parsley sprigs	1/8 teaspoon pepper
10 black peppercorns	1/2 cup unsifted all-purpose flour
1 bay leaf	
2 1/2 teaspoons salt	
1 lb carrots, pared and diced	Flaky pastry for 2-crust pie

1. In 6-quart kettle, place chicken, 8 cups water, celery, onion, lemon, parsley, peppercorns, bay leaf, and 2 teaspoons salt; bring to boiling. Reduce heat; simmer, covered, 2 hours, or until chicken is tender. Let chicken cool in broth.

2. Cut off meat in large pieces; cut into cubes. Strain broth, reserving 5 cups.

3. Meanwhile, in 1 inch boiling water, cook carrots and peas, covered, 15 minutes. Drain.

4. Toss vegetables with chicken and mushrooms, to combine. Divide mixture evenly among 8 (5 3/8-by-1 5/8-inch) deep-dish foil pans.

5. In medium saucepan, combine 4 cups reserved broth with cream, nutmeg, celery salt, pepper, and remaining salt; bring to boiling.

6. Combine flour with remaining broth, stirring to make a smooth paste; stir into boiling broth mixture. Reduce heat, and simmer 2 minutes, stirring constantly. Pour over chicken and vegetables; let cool completely.

7. Divide pastry into 8 parts. On lightly floured surface, roll each part into a 6-inch circle. Arrange a pastry round over filling in each pan; press edge of pastry to rim of pan, to seal. Freezer-wrap; label, and freeze until ready to use.

8. To bake pies: Preheat oven to 450F. Unwrap pies; make several gashes in center of each for steam vents; place on cookie sheet. Bake 40 minutes, or until crust is golden and filling is bubbling and hot.

MAKES 8 SERVINGS

*Or use 1 package (10 oz) frozen peas, partially thawed; do not cook.

FREEZER FRENCH BREAD

1 loaf French bread	Garlic salt, herbs, or poppy seed
Melted butter or margarine	

1. Make diagonal cuts in French bread at 1/2-inch intervals; be careful not to cut all the way through.

2. Brush cut sides with melted butter; sprinkle with garlic salt. Place in plastic bag; freeze until ready to use.

3. To serve: Preheat oven to 350F. Bake bread 20 minutes, or until heated through. Serve hot.

MAKES 1 LOAF

FROZEN PEPPERMINT ICE CREAM CAKE

1 pkg (15 oz) angel-food-cake mix	3/4 cup chopped walnuts
1/3 cup coarsely chopped thin chocolate-mint wafers	1/4 teaspoon peppermint extract
	3 pints soft vanilla ice cream*

1. Preheat oven to 375F.

2. Make cake as package label directs. Turn into ungreased 10-inch tube pan.

3. Bake on lowest shelf of oven 30 to 40 minutes, or until surface springs back when gently pressed with fingertip.

4. Invert pan immediately, hanging tube over neck of bottle. Let cool completely – about 1 hour. Remove; split crosswise into 3 layers.

5. In large bowl, add mints, nuts, and peppermint extract to ice cream, stirring until well combined. (If ice cream becomes too soft to spread, return to freezer for a few minutes.)

6. Working quickly, assemble cake on cookie sheet or foil: Spread bottom cake layer with 1/3 ice-cream mixture. Top with second cake layer; spread with 1/3 ice-cream mixture. Top with third cake layer; spread remaining ice-cream mixture over top.

7. Freeze until firm – about 2 hours. To serve: With sharp knife, cut frozen cake into slices.

MAKES 12 SERVINGS

Note: To store cake in freezer: Freeze as directed. Then freezer-wrap; label, and freeze.

*Or use peppermint ice cream; omit extract.

Crispy Oven-Fried Chicken*
Frozen French-Fried Potatoes
Frozen Mexican-Style Corn
Bibb Lettuce Salad
with Roquefort Dressing
Hot Corn Muffins
Frozen Pineapple Dessert*
Coffee   Tea
SERVES 4

*Recipes given for starred dishes.

CRISPY OVEN-FRIED CHICKEN

2- to 2½-lb broiler fryer, cut up	1 teaspoon salt
¾ cup sour cream	⅛ teaspoon pepper
1 tablespoon lemon juice	½ teaspoon paprika
1 teaspoon Worcester-shire sauce	2 cloves garlic, finely chopped
1 teaspoon celery salt	1 cup packaged dry bread crumbs

1. Preheat oven to 350F. Grease a 13-by-9-by-2-inch baking dish. Wipe chicken with damp paper towels.
2. In medium bowl, combine sour cream with lemon juice, Worcestershire, celery salt, salt, pepper, paprika, and garlic; mix well.
3. Dip chicken into sour-cream mixture; then roll in bread crumbs, coating completely.
4. Arrange chicken pieces in baking dish; bake, uncovered, 45 to 60 minutes, or until chicken is tender and nicely browned.
5. Let chicken cool completely. Wrap in foil, individually or in a single layer; label, and freeze.
6. To reheat chicken: Preheat oven to 450F. Place wrapped frozen chicken in oven; bake 45 minutes.

(If chicken is individually wrapped, bake 30 minutes.)
7. Uncover chicken; bake 10 minutes longer, to crisp.
MAKES 4 SERVINGS

FROZEN PINEAPPLE DESSERT

3 egg yolks	3 egg whites
½ cup sugar	1 cup heavy cream
1 can (8¾ oz) crushed pineapple	1 cup vanilla-wafer crumbs (about 20 wafers)
2 teaspoons lemon juice	

1. In top of double boiler, with rotary beater, beat egg yolks with sugar until thick and lemon-colored.
2. Drain pineapple, reserving liquid. Gradually stir pineapple liquid and lemon juice into egg- yolk mixture.
3. Place over hot, not boiling, water. (Water in lower section should not touch upper part of double boiler.) Cook, stirring constantly, until the mixture thickens and coats a metal spoon – about 10 minutes.
4. Remove from heat. Stir in pineapple; cool until lukewarm.
5. In small bowl, beat egg whites until stiff peaks form. Beat cream until soft peaks form.
6. With wire whisk or rubber scraper, gently fold egg whites and cream into pineapple mixture.
7. Spread vanilla-wafer crumbs evenly over bottom of 1-quart refrigerator tray (or 2 small ones). Spread pineapple mixture evenly over crumbs.
8. Freeze until very firm – about 4 to 5 hours.
9. To serve, cut into thick slices or wedges.
MAKES 6 TO 8 SERVINGS

Serve-It-Buffet

Buffets are always fun. You can make them more fun by the food you serve and the way you serve it, too. Buffet food should be notable. And hot foods should be served hot – cold foods should be served cold. To accomplish this takes some planning. Here are some pointers to make your buffet a notable success. . . .

Avoid a traffic jam at the buffet table by arranging food and service logically; there should be no criss-crossing, no reaching accross the table, and no congestion. Stack plates at the "starting" end of the table. Menu should be simple, so that the complete meal can be placed on a large serving plate (except dessert and coffee, of course). Place silver and napkins close to each other at the "finishing" end of the table, ready to be picked up.

Water or wine is sometimes placed at the far end of the buffet table, or on a side table, for guests to take as they go by. Or you can wait until everyone is seated and pass the filled beverage glasses on a tray. At a card-table buffet, the water should be put on the tables before service begins.

Give your guests a place to put plates down. Individual snack tables set up with silver, glass, salt, and pepper on a pretty place mat are fine for small parties. Or for large affairs, use card tables for four, all decked in the same color cloths, with matching or contrasting napkins.

While the guests eat, the serving dishes should be refilled for second helpings. As guests finish, they get up and help themselves.

Dessert and coffee may be set up on a dessert cart, or on a side table, desk top, a chest of drawers, the top of a low bookcase, the top of a spinet piano, or any other flat surface, protected by a large tray. Or they may be placed on the main buffet table after the main course has been served.

Dessert plates and silver are on the table, and guests serve themselves, or the hostess may fill the plates and pass one to each guest. Coffee may be served along with or after the dessert. Coffeepot, coffee cups, saucers, sugar, and cream are arranged on the side table. When dessert and coffee cups are finished, the dessert plates, napkins, dirty ashtrays, and little tables are taken away.

If desired, a liqueur or cordial may be served. A tray with liqueur glasses is placed on the coffee table. Host or hostess serves each guest his preference.

Beauty Tips for Your Table

Your cloth should be gay, fascinating, colorful, rather than merely safe and proper. Though sometimes, of course, only a proper cloth will do, especially if you wish to focus attention on an eye-catching, conversation-making centerpiece.

Collect printed, plain, striped, or woven dress fabric, bed sheeting, upholstery material, dyed burlap, whatever you see that you're crazy about. They make stunning and unusual cloths for table or buffet.

If your cloth is patterned, use napkins in one or more solid colors, to accent colors in the design or to contrast sharply with it. Or, if your cloth is plain, use plaid, striped, or flowered napkins.

Choose a theme for your table appropriate to the season or the occasion, such as a holiday or the big game.

Food, silver, linen, and decorative objects on your table should blend with the character of the room in which you are serving.

Avoid the cluttered look of too many objects, too much color, too many flowers. Simplicity is the rule.

Collect good-looking, though not necessarily costly, pieces that will do double duty for serving: an urn that will hold flowers and double as a sugar bowl; a basket for rolls or potted plants; a salad bowl that could be used for your folded napkins.

Every hostess should have at least one great recipe with which to do a great occasion proud. We believe internationally famous Beef Stroganoff, tender, tasty, elegant, is such a one. Though the list of ingredients is long, the cooking time is short, and our way is easy.

Beef Stroganoff*
Wild and White Rice*
Fresh Asparagus, page 8
Lettuce and Watercress Salad Bowl
Warm French Bread
Fresh Strawberries in Port*
Chocolate Petit Fours
Coffee
SERVES 6

*Recipes given for starred dishes.

BEEF STROGANOFF

2 lb filet of beef	½ teaspoon salt
6 tablespoons butter or margarine	⅛ teaspoon pepper
1 cup chopped onion	1 can (10½ oz) condensed beef broth, undiluted
1 clove garlic, finely chopped	¼ cup dry white wine
½ lb fresh mushrooms, sliced ¼ inch thick	1 tablespoon snipped fresh dill
3 tablespoons all-purpose flour	1½ cups sour cream
2 teaspoons meat-extract paste (optional)	1½ cups cooked wild rice, below
1 tablespoon catsup	4 cups cooked white rice, below
	Fresh dill or parsley

1. Trim fat from beef. Cut filet crosswise into ½-inch-thick slices (photo a). Cut each slice, across grain, into ½-inch-wide strips.
2. Slowly heat large, heavy skillet. Melt 2 tablespoons butter. Add beef strips – just enough to cover skillet bottom. Over high heat, sear quickly on all sides. With tongs, remove beef as it browns (photo b). (It should be browned outside, rare inside.) Brown rest of beef; set aside.
3. In remaining hot butter in same skillet, sauté onion, garlic, and mushrooms until onion is golden – about 5 minutes. Remove from heat. Add flour, meat-extract paste, catsup, salt, and pepper; stir until smooth (photo c.) Gradually add broth; bring to boiling, stirring. Reduce heat; simmer 5 minutes.
4. Over low heat, add wine, the snipped fresh dill or dried dill, and sour cream, stirring until well combin-

ed (photo d.) Add beef; simmer just until sauce and beef are hot. Lightly toss wild and white rice.
5. Surround Stroganoff with rice. Snip 2 tablespoons fresh dill or 3 tablespoons parsley over the top (photo e).
MAKES 6 SERVINGS

WILD RICE

½ cup wild rice	½ teaspoon salt
3 cups cold water	

1. Wash rice several times; drain.
2. In medium saucepan, combine 3 cups cold water, salt, and rice; bring to boiling, covered. Boil, uncovered, 50 minutes, or until rice is tender.
3. Drain rice. Return to saucepan; heat very slowly 10 to 15 minutes.
MAKES ABOUT 1½ CUPS

OLD-FASHIONED FLUFFY WHITE RICE

1 tablespoon salt	1 cup long-grain white rice
2 quarts cold water	

1. In large saucepan over high heat, bring to boiling 2 quarts cold water and the salt.
2. Slowly add rice; boil, uncovered, about 20 minutes, or until rice is tender.
3. Drain well. Fluff up with fork.
MAKES 4 CUPS

FRESH STRAWBERRIES IN PORT

2 pint boxes fresh strawberries	1 cup red or white port wine
½ cup sugar	

1. Gently wash strawberries in cold water; drain; and hull.
2. In medium bowl, gently toss strawberries with sugar. Add wine.
3. Refrigerate at least 2 hours, stirring occasionally.
4. If desired, top individual servings with sweetened whipped cream.
MAKES 6 SERVINGS

a

b

c

e

d

Veal Marengo*
Parsleyed Potatoes   French Bread
Pickled Peppers, Carrots, and Mushrooms
Pavé*
Coffee
SERVES 12

*Recipes given for starred dishes.

VEAL MARENGO

½ cup salad oil	½ teaspoon dried
4 lb veal shoulder, cut in	rosemary leaves
1-inch cubes	2 teaspoons salt
1 cup chopped onion	½ teaspoon pepper
1 cup chopped celery	2 sprigs parsley
1 clove garlic, finely	1 lb fresh mushrooms,
chopped	sliced
1 cup dry white wine	2 tablespoons lemon
2 cans (8-oz size) tomato	juice
sauce	¼ cup butter or
2 bay leaves	margarine
1 teaspoon dried	
oregano leaves	Chopped parsley

1. Heat oil in 6-quart Dutch oven or kettle. Add veal cubes (about half at a time); sauté until browned all over. Remove veal as it browns. Continue until all veal is browned.
2. In same Dutch oven, cook onion, celery, and garlic, stirring, until onion is golden – about 5 minutes.
3. Stir in wine, tomato sauce, bay leaves, oregano, rosemary, salt, pepper, parsley, and veal.
4. Bring mixture to boiling; reduce heat; simmer, covered, 1½ hours, or until veal is tender. Remove bay leaves.
5. Meanwhile, toss mushrooms with lemon juice. In hot butter in medium skillet, sauté mushrooms until tender – about 5 minutes.
6. Add mushrooms to veal mixture; simmer, covered, 15 minutes longer.
7. To serve: Turn veal mixture into heated serving dish; sprinkle with chopped parsley.
MAKES 12 SERVINGS.
Note: Veal Marengo can be made a day ahead and refrigerated. Reheat slowly before serving.

PAVÉ

4 squares unsweetened	4 egg yolks
chocolate	¼ cup dark rum or
½ cup soft butter or	cognac
margarine	½ cup water
1 cup sifted	½ lb (20) ladyfingers,
confectioners' sugar	split

1. Melt chocolate in top of double boiler, over hot, not boiling, water. Cool slightly.
2. In medium bowl, combine butter, sugar, and egg yolks. With portable electric mixer, at high speed, beat mixture until smooth and fluffy.
3. At low speed, gradually add the melted chocolate, beating until well blended.
4. In shallow dish, combine rum with ½ cup water.
5. Dip ladyfingers into rum mixture; then arrange 10, cut side down, to make layer in center of narrow serving dish.
6. Using spatula, spread with one-fourth of chocolate mixture.
7. Continue to layer with remaining ladyfingers and chocolate mixture, making four layers in all.
8. Spread remaining chocolate mixture on sides and top; refrigerate 3 hours, or overnight.
9. To serve: Let stand at room temperature 10 minutes before slicing. Using sharp knife, cut into 16 (1-inch) slices.
MAKES 16 SERVINGS

Marinated Italian Peppers
Ripe Olives
Chicken-Breasts-and-Spaghetti Casserole*
Herbed Broccoli with Lemon Wedges*
Warm Italian Bread   Bread Sticks
Paris-Brest*
Coffee
SERVES 8

*Recipes given for starred dishes.

CHICKEN-BREASTS-AND-SPAGHETTI CASSEROLE

Sauce	1 teaspoon pepper
½ cup salad or olive oil	
1½ cups chopped onion	1½ pkg (1-lb size)
5 cloves garlic, finely	spaghetti
chopped	
⅓ cup chopped parsley	4 (12-oz size) broiler-fryer
2 cans (1-lb, 12-oz size)	breasts, halved
tomatoes, undrained	⅓ cup unsifted all-
4 cans (6-oz size) tomato	purpose flour
paste	1¼ teaspoons salt
2½ cups water	⅛ teaspoon pepper
1½ tablespoons dried	¼ cup butter or
oregano leaves	margarine, melted
2 teaspoons dried basil	½ cup grated Parmesan
leaves	cheese
2½ teaspoons salt	Finely chopped parsley

1. Day before the party, prepare sauce and spaghetti: Slowly heat oil in 6-quart kettle or Dutch oven. Add onion, garlic, and parsley; sauté, stirring, until onion is golden – about 5 minutes.

2. Stir in tomatoes, tomato paste, and 2½ cups water; bring to boiling. Reduce heat; simmer, uncovered, 15 minutes, stirring occasionally.

3. Add oregano, basil, salt, and pepper; simmer 45 minutes longer.

4. Meanwhile, cook spaghetti: For each ½ pound spaghetti, bring 3 quarts water and 1 tablespoon salt to a rapid boil. Add spaghetti; return to boiling; boil, uncovered, 10 minutes, or just until tender. Drain well.

5. Add 4 cups sauce to spaghetti; toss to mix well. Turn into 2 shallow 3-quart casseroles. Refrigerate, covered with foil, overnight. Also, refrigerate rest of sauce.

6. About 2 hours before serving, prepare chicken: Wipe chicken with damp paper towels. Combine flour, salt, and pepper; use to coat chicken.

7. In hot butter in large skillet, slowly sauté chicken until golden-brown on both sides.

8. Add 2 cups reserved sauce to spaghetti in each casserole, tossing to mix well.

9. Arrange 4 chicken-breast halves on spaghetti in each casserole; cover with rest of sauce. Cover tightly with foil; set aside.

10. About 1 hour before serving, preheat oven to 350F.

11. Bake casserole, covered, 45 to 60 minutes, until chicken is tender. Sprinkle each with cheese, then with parsley.

MAKES 8 SERVINGS

HERBED BROCCOLI

3 pkg (10-oz size) frozen broccoli spears	2 teaspoons dried marjoram leaves
Boiling water	8 lemon wedges
Salt	
⅓ cup butter or margarine, melted	

1. About 20 minutes before serving, cook broccoli as package label directs, in small amount of boiling, salted water. During cooking, slit any thick stems, so broccoli will cook more readily.

2. Drain broccoli. Arrange on serving platter.

3. Combine butter and marjoram; pour over broccoli. Garnish edge of platter with lemon wedges.

MAKES 8 SERVINGS

PARIS-BREST
(Cream Puff Ring)
(Pictured on page 30)

Cream Puff Dough, below	1 cup confectioners' sugar
1 egg yolk	2 teaspoons vanilla extract
1 tablespoon water	¼ teaspoon almond extract
⅓ cup sliced blanched almonds	
Chantilly	
2 cups heavy cream	Confectioners' sugar

1. Preheat oven to 400F. Make Cream Puff Dough. On baking sheet lined with waxed paper, draw an 8-inch circle.

2. Spoon dough into pastry bag with No. 8 star tip. Pipe an 8-inch circle of cream puff dough on prepared baking sheet, 1-inch wide.

3. Pipe a circle inside the 8-inch circle (be sure they touch each other). Pipe a third circle on top.

4. Bake 50 minutes. Meanwhile, mix egg yolk with 1 tablespoon water. Brush lightly over top (not side) of ring. Sprinkle with almonds.

5. Bake 10 minutes longer, or until ring is puffed and deep golden-brown. Remove to wire rack; let cool completely.

6. Meanwhile, make Chantilly: In medium bowl, combine cream, 1 cup confectioners' sugar, the vanilla and almond extracts; mix well. Refrigerate, covered, 1 hour, or until very well chilled. With electric beater, at high speed, beat until stiff.

7. To assemble Paris-Brest: With sharp knife, split ring in half crosswise. Scoop out any filaments of soft dough.

8. Place bottom of ring on serving plate. Fill with Chantilly piped through pastry tube with No. 8 tip. Set top ring in place; sprinkle with confectioners' sugar. Refrigerate if not serving at once.

MAKES 12 SERVINGS

CREAM PUFF DOUGH

½ cup butter or regular margarine	1 cup unsifted all-purpose flour
¼ teaspoon salt	4 eggs

1. In medium saucepan, combine 1 cup water, the butter, and salt. Bring to boiling over medium heat.

2. Remove from heat. Immediately, with a wooden spoon, beat in flour all at once.

3. Return to low heat, and continue beating until mixture forms a ball and leaves side of pan.

4. Remove from heat. Add eggs, one at a time, beating hard after each addition until smooth. Continue beating until the mixture is shiny and breaks in strands.

This golden pastry ring crowned with sliced almonds and confectioners' sugar takes its name— Paris-Brest—from the French train route on which it is believed to have first been served. The secret of its airy consistency is basic cream-puff dough, called *pâte à choux*, which is baked first, then split open and filled with whipped cream.

Beef in Burgundy*
with Gnocchi*
Chive-Buttered Julienne Carrots
Green Salad Bowl
Hot Assorted Rolls
Pears Sabayon*
Assorted Cookies
Coffee
SERVES 6

*Recipes given for starred dishes.

BEEF IN BURGUNDY

¼ cup butter or margarine	3 cups Burgundy
¼ cup salad oil	¼ teaspoon pepper
1¼ lb small white onions, peeled	2 bay leaves
4 lb chuck, trimmed, cut in 2-inch cubes	½ teaspoon dried thyme leaves
2½ tablespoons potato flour, or ¼ cup unsifted all-purpose flour	½ teaspoon dried marjoram leaves
1 teaspoon meat-extract paste (optional)	4 parsley sprigs
1 tablespoon tomato paste	¾ lb mushrooms, washed
	Chopped parsley

1. Preheat oven to 325F.
2. In 4-quart Dutch oven, heat butter and oil. In fat, sauté onions 5 minutes; remove.
3. Add beef, a third at a time, to fat; brown well on all sides, and remove.
4. Remove Dutch oven from heat; discard all but 1 tablespoon fat. Stir in the flour, meat- extract paste, and tomato paste until smooth.
5. Gradually add Burgundy, stirring until smooth. Then add beef, pepper, herbs, parsley sprigs, and mushrooms, stirring until well mixed.
6. Bake, covered, 1½ hours.
7. Add onions; bake 1 hour longer, or until meat is tender. Sprinkle with chopped parsley. Serve with Gnocchi.
MAKES 8 SERVINGS

GNOCCHI

1 cup water	4 eggs
½ cup butter or margarine	1 teaspoon dry mustard
1 cup sifted all-purpose flour	¼ cup grated Parmesan cheese
1 teaspoon salt	¼ cup butter or margarine, melted

1. In large saucepan, bring 1 cup water with butter to boiling. Remove from heat.

2. With spoon, beat in flour and salt.
3. Return to low heat. Continue beating until mixture forms ball.
4. Remove from heat; beat in eggs, one at a time, beating vigorously after each addition. Continue beating until dough is satiny. Stir in mustard and cheese.
5. Turn into large pastry bag, using a large, plain tube.
6. Fill 2-quart saucepan with water. Bring to boiling. Reduce heat.
7. Pipe cream puff mixture in a stream into hot water, cutting into 1-inch lengths as it drops into water. Gnocchi will rise to top as they are cooked. Drain well.
8. Arrange in shallow baking dish. Pour melted butter over top; run under broiler about 3 minutes, or until golden-brown.
MAKES 8 SERVINGS

PEARS SABAYON

1 cup granulated sugar	1 cup confectioners' sugar
3 cups water	
4 fresh pears, pared, halved, and cored*	¼ cup sherry
	¾ cup heavy cream

Sauce
4 egg yolks

1. In 4-quart saucepan, combine granulated sugar and 3 cups water; heat to melt sugar.
2. Add pears; cover; simmer gently until tender – about 30 minutes. Remove from heat.
3. Refrigerate pears in syrup several hours.
4. Make Sauce: In top of double boiler, with rotary beater or wire whisk, beat egg yolks, confectioners' sugar, and sherry until light.
5. Place over hot, not boiling, water; water should not touch bottom of double-boiler top. Cook, stirring constantly, 8 to 10 minutes.
6. Refrigerate 3 hours. Mixture thickens.
7. In medium bowl, beat cream until soft peaks form when beater is raised. Carefully fold in chilled sauce.
8. Drain pears. Serve topped with sauce.
MAKES 10 SERVINGS
*You may substitute large canned pear halves.

Blanquette de Veau*
Buttered Noodles
Tossed Green Salad Bowl
French Bread
Ginger Spongecake*
Coffee
SERVES 12

*Recipes given for starred dishes.

BLANQUETTE DE VEAU

3½ to 4 lb boneless veal shoulder, cut into 1½-inch cubes
2 cans (13¾-oz size) chicken broth
2 carrots, pared and cut into chunks
1 large, peeled whole onion
2 celery tops
1 leek
1 bouquet garni (see Note)
2 cloves garlic, peeled
5 tablespoons butter or margarine
18 to 20 peeled white onions, 1 inch in diameter
1 lb small fresh mushrooms, washed (if large cut into quarters)
3 tablespoons all-purpose flour
2 egg yolks
1 cup heavy cream
½ teaspoon salt
½ teaspoon white pepper
3 tablespoons fresh lemon juice
1 to 2 tablespoons chopped parsley

1. In 5-quart Dutch oven, cover veal cubes with cold water; bring to boiling over high heat; boil rapidly 1 minute. Drain veal.

2. Wash Dutch oven. Put back veal; add 3⅓ cups chicken broth, the carrot, 1 large onion, the celery, leek, bouquet garni and garlic. Bring to boiling over medium heat; skim surface if necessary. Reduce heat; simmer veal, covered, 1 to 1½ hours, or until tender.

3. While veal is cooking, add water to remaining chicken broth to measure ⅔ cup. Combine with 2 tablespoons butter and the onions in a large skillet. Bring to boiling; reduce heat and simmer, covered 20 minutes, or until onions are tender. With slotted spoon, remove onions to bowl. Add mushrooms to broth in skillet; bring to boiling; reduce heat and simmer, covered, 5 minutes. With slotted spoon, lift mushrooms to bowl. Add stock remaining in skillet to Dutch oven.

4. When veal is tender, remove with slotted spoon to bowl with onions and mushrooms. Keep warm.

5. Strain the stock from Dutch oven into a quart measure – there should be almost a full 3 cups. (Discard the large onion, the carrot, celery tops and leek.) Skim fat from surface.

6. In large saucepan, melt remaining butter over medium heat. Remove from heat; stir in flour until smooth. Cook, stirring over low heat about 2 minutes, or until golden. Do not brown flour. Remove from heat; stir in 3 cups stock with a wire whisk. Bring to boiling, stirring constantly; reduce heat and simmer 10 minutes, stirring occasionally. Remove from heat.

7. In medium bowl, blend egg yolks and cream with wire whisk. With whisk, beat in sauce mixture, a little at a time, until about ⅔ cup has been added. Then pour all of egg-yolk-cream mixture into the saucepan, stirring with wire whisk.

8. Bring to boiling, stirring, about 1 minute, or until thickened. Stir in salt, pepper and lemon juice.

9. Drain veal, onions and mushrooms of any liquid. Spoon onto serving platter. Pour sauce over all. Sprinkle with the chopped parsley. Serve at once.
MAKES 8 SERVINGS
Note: For bouquet garni, tie a large sprig of fresh parsley, ½ teaspoon dried thyme leaves and a bay leaf in a square of cheesecloth, to make a small bag.

GINGER SPONGECAKE

Cake
6 egg whites
1¾ cups sifted all-purpose flour
½ teaspoon salt
2 teaspoons ground ginger
1½ cups granulated sugar
6 egg yolks
2 tablespoons grated lemon peel
2 tablespoons lemon juice
¼ cup water

Apricot Glaze
½ cup dried apricots
¼ cup granulated sugar
½ cup water

Frosting
2 to 3 tablespoons light cream
2 cups sifted confectioners' sugar

1. Make Cake: In large bowl of mixer, let egg whites warm to room temperature – 1 hour.

2. Meanwhile, preheat oven to 350F. Sift flour and salt with ginger. Set aside.

3. With electric mixer at medium speed, beat egg whites until foamy. Gradually beat in ½ cup sugar, beating well after each addition.

4. Continue beating until soft peaks form when beater is slowly raised. Set aside.

5. In small bowl of electric mixer, at high speed, with the same beaters, beat egg yolks until thick and lemon-colored.

6. Gradually beat in remaining sugar; continue beating until mixture is smooth and well blended – about 5 minutes.

7. At low speed, add flour mixture, lemon peel, lemon juice, and ¼ cup water, guiding mixture into beaters with rubber spatula, beating just until combined – about 1 minute.

8. With wire whisk or rubber spatula, using an

under-and-over motion, gently fold egg-yolk mixture into egg whites just until blended.

9. Turn into ungreased 10-inch tube pan. Bake about 40 minutes, or until cake tester inserted in center comes out clean.

10. Invert pan immediately, hanging tube over neck of bottle. Let cool completely.

11. Meanwhile, make Apricot Glaze: With scissors dipped in water, cut apricots into small pieces. In small saucepan, combine apricots, sugar, and 1/2 cup water; simmer covered, 10 minutes, or until apricots are tender and mixture thickens. Mash apricots with back of spoon. Let glaze cool.

12. Make Frosting: In small bowl, stir enough cream into confectioners' sugar to make frosting thin enough to spread; stir until smooth.

13. Turn out cake onto cake plate. Spread glaze over top; then spoon frosting over glaze, letting some run down side.

MAKES 12 SERVINGS

Ragout of Beef with Walnuts*
Buttered Noodles
Tomato-Cucumber Salad
Toasted Sesame Sticks*
Iced Zabaione*
Coffee
SERVES 6 TO 8

*Recipes given for starred dishes.

RAGOUT OF BEEF WITH WALNUTS

1/2 cup salad oil	1 tablespoon salt
18 small white onions, peeled	1/2 teaspoon pepper
1 clove garlic, slivered	1 cup walnut halves
3 lb chuck, cut in 1-inch cubes	3 cups thinly sliced celery
1 cup dry red wine	1/4 cup unsifted all-purpose flour
1/4 teaspoon dried thyme leaves	1/2 cup water
4 sprigs parsley	
2 bay leaves	Cooked noodles
1 can (10 1/2 oz) beef consommé, undiluted	

1. In 1/4 cup hot oil in 4-quart Dutch oven or kettle, sauté the onions and garlic until golden – about 10 minutes. Remove from Dutch oven.

2. Heat remaining oil in Dutch oven. Add chuck; brown well on all sides – takes about 20 minutes.

3. Add wine, thyme, parsley sprigs, bay leaves, consommé, salt, and pepper; mix well.

4. Bring mixture to boiling; reduce heat; simmer, covered, 1 hour.

5. Return onion and garlic to Dutch oven; cook, covered, 30 minutes.

6. Add walnuts and celery; continue cooking, covered, 30 minutes longer, or until beef is tender.

7. In small bowl, combine flour with 1/2 cup water to make a smooth paste.

8. Gradually add flour to meat mixture. Cook, stirring, until ragout is smooth and thickened.

9. Serve hot, over noodles. Sprinkle with chopped parsley, if desired.

MAKES 6 TO 8 SERVINGS

Note: Ragout may be cooked a day ahead and refrigerated. Reheat before serving.

TOASTED SESAME STICKS

3 frankfurter rolls	1/2 cup sesame seed
1/3 cup soft butter or margarine	

1. Preheat oven to 400F.

2. Cut rolls in half lengthwise; then cut each half crosswise into fourths.

3. Spread three sides of each roll with butter; then dip into sesame seed.

4. Place, on ungreased cookie sheet; bake 15 minutes, or until golden-brown.

MAKES 24.

ICED ZABAIONE

1 teaspoon unflavored gelatine	2 cups heavy cream
1/2 cup sugar	1 teaspoon vanilla extract
1/4 cup water	Chopped toasted almonds (optional)
8 egg yolks	
3/4 cup sherry or Marsala	

1. In top of double boiler, combine gelatine and sugar; stir in 1/4 cup water.

2. Add egg yolks; with portable mixer, at high speed, beat until light and fluffy.

3. Gradually add sherry, beating constantly, at medium speed, until well blended.

4. Over hot, not boiling, water, continue beating about 8 minutes, or until mixture just begins to hold its shape.

5. Remove from water; cool; then refrigerate until cold – about 1 hour.

6. In large bowl, whip cream and vanilla until cream is stiff enough to hold its shape.

7. Fold in cooled egg mixture, with wire whisk or rubber spatula, using an under-and-over motion, mixing until blended.

8. Spoon into 8 sherbet glasses. Cover top of each glass with foil; freeze until firm – about 2 hours.

9. To serve: Remove foil; garnish top of each serving. If desired, with chopped toasted almonds.

MAKES 8 SERVINGS.

Crabmeat Salad with Remoulade Sauce*
Sliced Tomatoes
Hot Biscuits   Butter Curls
Graham-Crumb Torte*
Coffee
SERVES 8

*Recipes given for starred dishes.

CRABMEAT SALAD
WITH REMOULADE SAUCE

3 cans (6½-oz size)
   crabmeat, drained
2 cups thinly sliced
   celery

Remoulade Sauce
1 clove garlic, crushed
1 teaspoon dried
   tarragon leaves
¼ cup chopped parsley
2 hard-cooked eggs,
   coarsely chopped
1½ cups mayonnaise or
   cooked salad dressing

1 teaspoon salt
2 tablespoons capers,
   drained
½ teaspoon anchovy
   paste
1 teaspoon dry mustard
1 tablespoon lemon juice

Watercress
2 tomatoes, peeled and
   liced
½ cucumber, thinly
   sliced

1. In medium bowl, separate crabmeat pieces, removing membrane.
2. Add celery; toss lightly to combine. Cover; refrigerate until serving time.
3. Meanwhile, make Remoulade Sauce: In large bowl, combine all sauce ingredients, mixing until well blended.
4. Reserve ½ cup sauce. To remaining sauce, add the crabmeat-celery mixture, mixing gently. Refrigerate, covered, 1 hour.
5. To serve: Mound crabmeat salad in center of chilled salad platter. Put watercress around salad. Garnish with tomato and cucumber slices. Pass remaining sauce.
MAKES 6 TO 8 SERVINGS

GRAHAM-CRUMB TORTE

Torte
5 egg whites
1½ cups packaged
   graham-cracker
   crumbs
1 teaspoon baking
   powder
½ teaspoon salt
1 cup finely chopped
   walnuts or pecans
1 cup sugar
5 egg yolks
1 teaspoon vanilla
   extract

Filling
¼ cup sugar
2 tablespoons
   cornstarch
⅛ teaspoon salt
1 cup milk
2 egg yolks, slightly
   beaten
1 teaspoon vanilla
   extract

½ cup heavy cream,
   whipped

¼ cup coarsely chopped
   walnuts or pecans

1. Make Torte: In large bowl of electric mixer, let egg whites warm to room temperature – about 1 hour.
2. In medium bowl, combine graham-cracker crumbs, baking powder, salt, and nuts; mix well. Set aside.
3. Preheat oven to 350F. Line bottoms of 2 (9-by-1¾-inch) layer-cake pans with waxed paper; lightly grease lining.
4. With electric mixer at medium speed, beat egg whites until soft peaks form when beater is slowly raised. Gradually add ¼ cup sugar, 1 tablespoon at a time, beating well after each addition.
5. Continue beating until shiny, stiff peaks form when beater is slowly raised.
6. In small bowl of electric mixer, at high speed, using the same beaters, beat egg yolks until thick and lemon-colored.
7. Gradually beat in remaining ¾ cup sugar, 2 tablespoons at a time; continue beating until smooth and well blended – about 5 minutes. Add vanilla.
8. Add egg yolks to graham-crumb mixture, mixing until well blended.
9. With rubber spatula, using and under-and-over motion, fold egg-yolk mixture into beaten egg whites just until combined.
10. Turn into prepared pans; spread evenly. Bake 25 to 30 minutes, or until surface springs back when gently pressed with fingertip.
11. Invert torte by hanging each pan between two other pans; let cool completely before removing from pans.
12. To remove from pans: Run spatula around edge of pan; turn out layers; peel off waxed paper.
13. Make Filling: In small, heavy saucepan, combine sugar with cornstarch and salt.
14. Gradually stir in milk. Over medium heat, bring to boiling, stirring; boil 1 minute. Remove from heat.
15. Add half of hot mixture to egg yolks; mix well. Gradually return to saucepan, stirring constantly.
16. Bring back to boiling, stirring. Remove from heat; add vanilla. Cool completely. Cover surface with square of waxed paper; refrigerate 1 hour.
17. Put torte layers together with filling. Spread whipped cream on top; sprinkle with chopped nuts. Refrigerate at least 2 hours before serving.
MAKES 8 TO 10 SERVINGS

Bengal Curry*
Curry Accompaniments
Pineapple Rice*
Baked Tomato Halves*
Hot Buttered Rolls
Chocolate-Rum Cake*
Coffee
SERVES 8

Recipes given for starred dishes.

BENGAL CURRY

Curry
1/4 cup shortening
4 lb chuck, cut into 1-inch cubes
1 cup sliced onion
2 tablespoons curry powder
2 teaspoons salt
1/4 teaspoon pepper
1/4 teaspoon ground cloves
1/4 cup slivered crystallized ginger
2 tablespoons chopped fresh mint leaves, or 1 teaspoon dried mint leaves

1/4 cup unsifted all-purpose flour
3 cans (10 1/2-oz size) beef broth, undiluted
1 cup canned flaked coconut
1/4 cup lime juice
1 cup light cream

Pineapple Rice, below

Curry Accompaniments
Chopped cashew nuts, chopped unpared cucumber, prepared chutney, preserved kumquats

1. Day before the party, make Curry: In hot shortening in large Dutch oven, sauté beef cubes, turning, until browned all over – about 20 minutes. Remove the beef cubes as they brown.
2. In 2 tablespoons drippings in Dutch oven, sauté onion, curry powder, salt, pepper, cloves, ginger, and mint. Cook, stirring, until onion is tender – about 5 minutes.
3. Remove from heat. Add flour, stirring until well combined. Gradually stir in broth.
4. Return beef to Dutch oven; bring to boiling. Reduce heat; simmer, covered, 1 1/2 hours, or until beef is tender.
5. Remove from heat; let cool. Refrigerate, covered, overnight.
6. Also, make Pineapple Rice, below.
7. About 40 minutes before serving, let curry stand at room temperature 15 minutes. Prepare Curry Accompaniments. Put each into a small serving bowl.

8. Over medium heat, gently reheat curry, stirring occasionally, about 20 minutes, or until heated through. Stir in coconut, lime juice, and cream; heat gently about 5 minutes.
9. Turn into chafing dish. Serve along with Pineapple Rice, surrounded by Curry Accompaniments.
MAKES 8 SERVINGS

PINEAPPLE RICE

2 1/2 cups long-grain white rice
2 1/2 teaspoons salt
1/4 cup water

2 1/2 tablespoons butter or margarine
1 can (8 1/2 oz) crushed pineapple, drained

1. Day before the party, cook rice: In 3-quart heavy saucepan, combine rice with 1 quart cold water and the salt.
2. Over high heat; simmer, covered, 12 to 14 minutes, or until liquid is absorbed and rice is tender. If necessary, drain rice.
4. Refrigerate, covered, overnight.
5. About 40 minutes before serving, preheat oven to 300F. Turn rice into a 15 1/2-by-10 1/2-by- 1-inch pan; fluff it up with fork.
6. Sprinkle with 1/4 cup water. Heat, covered with foil, 30 minutes, stirring several times with fork.
7. Add butter and pineapple; toss, with fork, to mix well.
MAKES 8 SERVINGS

BAKED TOMATO HALVES

4 large tomatoes (about 2 1/4 lb)
3 tablespoons butter or margarine, melted
3/4 teaspoon seasoned salt
1 1/4 teaspoons garlic powder

1 1/2 teaspoons ground coriander
1 1/2 teaspoons ground cumin
1/2 cup packaged dry bread crumbs

1. Day before the party, prepare tomatoes: Wash; remove stems; cut tomatoes in half crosswise.
2. In small bowl, combine butter with remaining ingredients, mixing well.
3. Spread cut surface of each tomato half with butter mixture. Place, in single layer, in shallow baking dish. Refrigerate, covered, overnight.
4. About 40 minutes before serving, preheat oven to 300F.* Let tomatoes stand at room temperature 10 minutes.
5. Bake, uncovered, 30 minutes, or until golden on top.
MAKES 8 SERVINGS
*Bake in oven along with Pineapple Rice.

CHOCOLATE-RUM CAKE

Cake
1 pkg (1 lb, 3 oz) yellow-
   cake mix
2 eggs
1 tablespoon grated
   orange peel

Frosting
4 squares unsweetened
   chocolate
1 cup sifted
   confectioners' sugar
2 eggs
1 tablespoon white rum

1 tablespoon orange
   juice

Rum-Cream Filling
2 teaspoons unflavored
   gelatine
2 tablespoons water
2 cups heavy cream
1/2 cup sifted
   confectioners' sugar
1/3 cup white rum
1 cup coarsely chopped
   walnuts

1. Day before the party, make and frost cake: Preheat oven to 350F. Lightly grease and flour 2 (9-inch) layer-cake pans.
2. Make cake mix as package label directs, using eggs, orange peel, and water specified on package.
3. Turn into prepared pans; bake about 30 minutes, or until surface springs back when gently pressed with fingertip.
4. Let cool in pans 10 minutes. Turn out onto wire racks; let cool completely.
5. Make Frosting: Melt chocolate over hot, not boiling water. With wooden spoon, beat in confectioners' sugar alternately with eggs. Beat in rum and orange juice; continue beating until smooth. Set aside.
6. Make the Rum-Cream Filling: Sprinkle gelatine over 2 tablespoons water; let stand 5 minutes, to soften. Set in pan of hot water; heat, stirring, until gelatine is dissolved.
7. With rotary beater, beat cream with sugar just until slightly stiff. Gradually beat in rum and gelatine until mixture is stiff.
8. To assemble the cake: Halve each layer crosswise.
9. On cake plate, put layers together with Rum-Cream Filling. Frost top and side with Frosting.
10. Press walnuts around side of cake, covering completely. Refrigerate until serving – overnight, if desired, or at least 1 hour.
MAKES 10 SERVINGS

Buffets for Special Occasions

LADIES-CLUB LUNCHEON BUFFET
Pâté-Stuffed Chicken Breasts en Gelée*
Vegetables Parisienne*
Almond Tart*
Coffee
SERVES 8

Recipes given for starred dishes.

PÂTÉ-STUFFED CHICKEN BREASTS EN GELÉE

1 large onion, sliced
2 celery stalks, sliced
2 carrots, sliced
2 parsley sprigs
1 1/2 teaspoon salt
1/2 teaspoon dried thyme
   leaves
2 small bay leaves
2 cans (10 3/4-oz size)
   condensed chicken
   broth, undiluted
1 cup water
5 (1-lb size) whole chick-
   en breasts, split in half
Wine Aspic, page 37

2 cans (4 3/4-oz size) liver
   pâté

Glaze
1 env unflavored gelatine
1/4 cup cold water
1 cup heavy cream

Chives, cucumber,
   radishes, carrots,
   black olives and
   capers, to make
   flowers
Clear Glaze, page 37
Watercress sprigs

1. In 6-quart kettle, combine onion, celery, carrot, parsley, salt, thyme, bay leaves, undiluted chicken broth, 1 cup water and the split chicken breasts; bring to boiling.
2. Reduce heat and simmer, covered, 30 minutes, or just until chicken is fork-tender.
3. Remove kettle from heat; let the chicken cool in broth. Meanwhile, make Wine Aspic.
4. Remove chicken from broth; reserve broth. Remove and discard skin and bone from chicken breasts; trim edges evenly.
5. On underside of each chicken breast, spread about 1 tablespoon liver pâté, mounding it slightly. Refrigerate chicken breasts, covered, 1 hour.

6. Meanwhile, strain broth; skim off fat. Reserve 2 cups broth.

7. Make Glaze: In medium saucepan, bring reserved broth to boiling. Reduce heat; simmer, uncovered, 30 minutes, or until reduced to 1 cup.

8. In ¼ cup cold water in medium bowl, let gelatine stand 5 minutes, to soften. Add hot broth, stirring to dissolve gelatine.

9. Add heavy cream, mixing until well combined with gelatine mixture.

10. Set bowl with gelatine mixture in ice water; let stand about 20 minutes, or until well chilled but not thickened. Stir occasionally. Remove from ice water.

11. Place chicken breasts, pâté side down, on a wire rack; set rack on a tray. Spoon glaze over chicken breasts.

12. Refrigerate on tray for 30 minutes, or until glaze is set.

13. Scrape glaze from tray; reheat and set in saucepan in ice water again to chill. Spoon glaze over chicken breasts, coating completely.

14. To make decoration: Use chives for stems. Cut skin from cucumber with sharp knife to make leaves. Use radish skin, thin slices of partially cooked carrot and thin slices of black olive, cut with small aspic cutter or sharp knife, for flowers. Use capers for flower centers. Press flowers into glaze, to decorate. Refrigerate until glaze is set – about 1 hour. Meanwhile, make Clear Glaze. Spoon Clear Glaze on top to cover completely. Refrigerate 1 hour longer.

15. To serve: Arrange chicken breasts, in a single layer, on chilled serving platter. Decorate platter with Wine Aspic and watercress.

MAKES 10 SERVINGS

WINE ASPIC

3 env unflavored gelatine
2 cans (13¾-oz size) chicken broth
3 tablespoons lemon juice
½ cup dry white wine
¼ teaspoon liquid gravy seasoning

1. Sprinkle gelatine over 1 cup chicken broth in small saucepan; let stand 5 minutes to soften.

2. Stir over medium heat to dissolve gelatine. Add remaining chicken broth, lemon juice, wine and liquid gravy seasoning.

3. Strain into a 13-by-9-by-2-inch pan. Refrigerate until firm – 3 hours or overnight.

4. Cut firm gelatine into eight crosswise strips; cut 2 strips to make 10 triangles. Cut remaining gelatine into cubes.

5. Use triangles to decorate outside of platter; mound cubes in center.

CLEAR GLAZE

¼ cup cold water
1 env unflavored gelatine
1 can (13¾ oz) chicken broth

1. In ¼ cup cold water in medium bowl, let gelatine stand 5 minutes, to soften. Heat broth; add to gelatine mixture, stirring to dissolve gelatine.

2. Set bowl with gelatine mixture in ice water; let stand about 20 minutes, or until well chilled but not thickened, stirring occasionally. Remove from ice water. Use to glaze decorated chicken breasts.

VEGETABLES PARISIENNE

1 cup mayonnaise
¼ cup lemon juice
3 pkg (10-oz size) frozen petits pois
4 large stalks celery, cut on diagonal, ½ inch thick
1 lb small carrots, pared and cut in ½-inch rounds
Chopped parsley

1. Combine the mayonnaise and lemon juice; mix well. Refrigerate, covered, to chill well – several hours.

2. Meanwhile, prepare vegetables: Cook peas as package label directs. Do not overcook. Then plunge into ice water to cool rapidly. Drain well; pat dry on paper towels. Refrigerate.

3. In medium saucepan, bring ½ cup water to boiling; add celery. Simmer, covered, 5 minutes, or until just tender. Chill in ice water and dry well, as in step 2. Refrigerate.

4. Following directions for cooking celery, cook carrots about 8 minutes, or until just tender. Chill and drain well, as above. Refrigerate.

5. At serving time, combine vegetables in chilled bowl; toss with mayonnaise mixture. Sprinkle with parsley.

MAKES ABOUT 16 SERVINGS

ALMOND TART

Pastry

1 cup sifted all-purpse
   flour
¼ cup sugar
2 teaspoons grated
   lemon peel
⅓ cup butter or
   margarine
1 egg yolk

¾ cup sugar
1 tablespoon grated
   orange peel
½ teaspoon almond
   extract
1½ cups heavy cream
1 cup blanched almonds,
   ground
¼ cup finely chopped
   almond macaroons

Filling

3 egg yolks, slightly
   beaten
⅓ cup water

Citron or angelica
   (optional)

1. Make Pastry: Combine flour, sugar, and lemon peel in medium bowl.
2. With pastry blender or 2 knives, cut in butter until mixture resembles coarse cornmeal.
3. Stir in egg yolk.
4. With hands, mix pastry until well blended.
5. Press evenly onto bottom and side of 9-inch pie plate, but not on rim. Refrigerate 1 hour.
6. Preheat oven to 350F.
7. Make Filling: In medium bowl, combine egg yolks, ⅓ cup water, and remaining filling ingredients. Beat, with rotary beater, until mixture is smooth.
8. Pour into prepared pie shell; bake about 45 to 50 minutes, or just until filling is set in center. (Shake pie gently; center should be firm.)
9. Let cool completely on wire rack. Refrigerate until chilled – 2 hours.
10. Serve garnished, if desired, with strips of citron or angelica.
MAKES 8 SERVINGS

BEFORE-THE-BIG-GAME BUFFET
Smorgasbord Sandwiches*
Pickled Beets*
Marinated Cucumbers*
McCall's Best Chocolate Loaf Cake*
Carbonated Beverages   Milk
SERVES 6

Recipes given for starred dishes.

SMORGASBORD SANDWICHES

1. Arrange a bed of crisp salad greens on a large platter.

2. Place 1 pound assorted sliced cheeses (Swiss, Muenster, caraway) and 1 pound of cold cuts (head cheese, bologna, smoked tongue, ham, roast beef or pork) on greens – cheeses at one end and meat at other end of platter.
3. Garnish center of platter with watercress and radishes.
4. Place serving platter on buffet table with basket of assorted breads; pots of prepared mustard, catsup, and horseradish; and bowls of Pickled Beets and Marinated Cucumbers.
MAKES 6 SERVINGS

PICKLED BEETS

1 jar (1 lb) sliced beets
1 cup vinegar
¼ cup sugar
1 teaspoon salt

Dash ground cloves
1 bay leaf
1 medium onion, thinly
   sliced

1. Drain beets, reserving ½ cup liquid; turn beets into serving dish.
2. In small saucepan, combine beet liquid and remaining ingredients; bring to boiling point. Reduce heat; simmer 5 minutes. Pour over beets.
3. Refrigerate until well chilled – 1 hour.
MAKES ABOUT 2 CUPS

MARINATED CUCUMBERS

2 small cucumbers
   (or 1 large cucumber),
   unpeeled, very thinly
   sliced
2 teaspoons salt

¼ cup finely chopped
   parsley
½ cup vinegar
½ teaspoon sugar
Dash pepper

1. In an 8- or 9-inch pie plate, layer cucumber slices with 1 teaspoon salt.
2. With another pie plate, press cucumbers, to extract water and make cucumbers wilt.
3. Refrigerate about 1 hour.
4. Pour off the salt water. Sprinkle parsley, vinegar, sugar, pepper, and remaining salt over cucumbers. Toss to mix well.
MAKES ABOUT 2 CUPS

McCALL'S BEST CHOCOLATE LOAF CAKE

1 cup boiling water
2 squares unsweetened
   chocolate, cut up
2 cups sifted all-purpose
   flour
1 teaspoon baking soda
¼ teaspoon salt
½ cup butter or
   margarine, softened

1 teaspoon vanilla
   extract
1½ cups light-brown
   sugar, firmly packed
2 eggs
½ cup sour cream

1. In small bowl, pour boiling water over chocolate; let cool.
2. Meanwhile, preheat oven to 325F. Grease well and flour a 9-by-5-by-3-inch loaf pan.
3. Sift flour with baking soda and salt; set aside.
4. In large bowl of electric mixer, at high speed, beat butter, vanilla, sugar, and eggs until light and fluffy, about 5 minutes, occasionally scraping side of bowl with rubber spatula.
5. At low speed, beat in flour mixture (in fourths), alternately with sour cream (in thirds), beginning and ending with flour mixture.
6. Beat in chocolate mixture just until combined.
7. Pour batter into prepared pan. Bake 60 to 70 minutes, or until cake tester inserted in center comes out clean.
8. Cool in pan 15 minutes. Remove from pan; cool thoroughly on wire rack. Frost with Milk-Chocolate Frosting, below.

MILK-CHOCOLATE FROSTING

2 squares unsweetened chocolate	1 egg
2 tablespoons butter or margarine, softened	1/4 cup milk
1 cup sifted confectioners' sugar	1 teaspoon vanilla extract

1. Melt chocolate over hot water; let cool.
2. In small bowl, with portable electric mixer, at medium speed, or wooden spoon, beat butter, sugar, egg, milk, and vanilla until smooth.
3. Stir in chocolate.
4. Set bowl of frosting in ice water. Beat until frosting is smooth and barely holds its shape.
MAKES ENOUGH TO FROST A 9-INCH SQUARE CAKE, OR A 13-BY-9-BY-2-INCH OBLONG CAKE; OR A LOAF CAKE

HOUSEWARMING BUFFET
Cream of Curry Soup*
Rock Cornish Hens on the Spit*
Tossed Green Salad
Hot Rolls
Apple Raisin Turnovers*
Coffee
SERVES 8

*Recipes given for starred dishes.

CREAM OF CURRY SOUP

2 tablespoons butter or margarine	2 cans (13 3/4-oz size) clear chicken broth
2 tablespoons finely chopped onion	4 egg yolks, slightly beaten
2 teaspoons curry powder	1 cup heavy cream
1 tablespoon all-purpose flour	1 cup canned crushed pineapple, well drained

1. In hot butter in large skillet, sauté onion until golden – about 5 minutes.
2. Remove from heat. Stir in curry powder and flour until smooth. Add chicken broth; bring to boiling, stirring.
3. Blend some of hot broth mixture into egg yolks; then stir into broth in skillet.
4. Cook, stirring, over low heat, about 1 minute, or until slightly thickened.
5. Strain into large bowl; let cool.
6. Refrigerate, covered, several hours. Just before serving, stir in cream and pineapple.
MAKES 7 OR 8 SERVINGS

ROCK CORNISH HENS ON THE SPIT

1 1/2 cups finely chopped onion	1/2 teaspoon dried marjoram leaves
1 cup finely chopped celery	1/2 teaspoon rubbed sage
1/2 cup finely chopped parsley	1 teaspoon salt
1/2 lb butter or margarine, melted	1/4 teaspoon pepper
6 cups small day-old bread cubes	1 cup chopped prepared chutney, undrained
1 teaspoon dried thyme leaves	8 (1-lb size) Rock Cornish game hens

1. Preheat rotisserie to 400F (or oven to 350F).
2. In medium skillet, sauté onion, celery, and parsley in 1/2 cup butter until tender. Remove from heat.
3. In large bowl, combine sautéed vegetables with bread cubes, seasonings and chutney.
4. Stuff each hen with about 3/4 cup dressing. Close opening with wooden picks; truss with string.
5. Thread hens on spit; secure with prongs. (Or place, breast side up, in shallow roasting pan without rack.) Brush hens with 4 tablespoons butter.
6. Secure spit in rotisserie; roast hens 30 minutes, basting once with remaining butter. (Or roast in oven 45 to 50 minutes, basting once with remaining butter.) When done, drumstick can be easily moved.
7. To serve, remove wooden picks and string.
MAKES 8 SERVINGS

APPLE-RAISIN TURNOVERS

Pastry for 2-crust pie	¼ teaspoon ground nutmeg
Filling	¼ cup seedless raisins
1 can (1 lb, 4 oz) sliced apples, drained and chopped	1 tablespoon grated orange peel (optional)
¼ cup sugar	1 egg white
1 tablespoon all-purpose flour	1 tablespoon water
¼ teaspoon ground cinnamon	2 tablespoons sugar

1. Prepare pastry; form into a ball. Wrap in waxed paper, and refrigerate. Preheat oven to 425F.
2. Make Filling: In medium bowl, combine all ingredients; mix well.
3. On lightly floured surface, roll pastry into an 18-by-9-inch rectangle. Cut rectangle into eight 4½-inch squares. Moisten edges of each square.
4. Spread 2 tablespoons filling on half of each square; fold over; seal edges with tines of fork. Prick top of each in 3 places with fork.
5. Beat egg white slightly with 1 tablespoon water; use to brush turnovers. Sprinkle each with a little of the sugar.
6. Bake, on ungreased cookie sheet, about 20 minutes, or until crust is golden-brown.
7. Cool partially on wire rack; serve warm.
MAKES 8

A THANKSGIVING BUFFET
Corn and Clam Chowder*
Roast Turkey* with
Brazil-Nut Stuffing*
Giblet Gravy
Fresh Cranberry Jelly*
Stuffed Acorn Squash*
Orange and Endive Salad
Brandied-Mincemeat Pie*
Grapes   Nuts
Coffee
SERVES 8

*Recipes given for starred dishes.

CORN AND CLAM CHOWDER

3 slices bacon, cut up	1 can (12 oz) whole-kernel corn
1½ cups chopped onion	
2 tablespoons butter or margarine	2 cups diced, pared potato
2 tablespoons all-purpose flour	1 teaspoon salt
2 cans (8-oz size) minced clams or 1½ dozen fresh clams	⅛ teaspoon black pepper
	Water

1. In 6-quart Dutch oven or kettle, sauté bacon slightly. Add onion and butter, and sauté until onion is golden – about 5 minutes. Remove from heat. Add flour, stirring until smooth.
2. Drain canned or fresh clams, reserving liquid. Chop fresh clams coarsely. Drain corn, reserving liquid.
3. Add clams, corn, potato, salt, pepper to Dutch oven. Combine clam and corn liquids; add water to measure 4 cups. Add to Dutch oven.
4. Bring to boiling; reduce heat, and simmer, covered, 25 to 30 minutes, or until potato is tender. Serve hot.
MAKES 7 CUPS; 6 TO 8 SERVINGS

ROAST TURKEY WITH BRAZIL-NUT STUFFING

10-lb ready-to-cook turkey	1 carrot, quartered
Brazil-Nut Stuffing, page 41	Water
	⅓ cup unsifted all-purpose flour
½ cup butter or margarine, melted	1 to 2 teaspoons meat-extract paste (optional)
Giblets and neck from turkey	⅛ teaspoon pepper
1 onion, quartered	

1. Preheat oven to 450F.
2. Stuff and, if necessary, truss turkey. Brush with melted butter. Wrap turkey in heavy-duty aluminum foil, so it is completely covered.
3. Place on rack in shallow roasting pan; roast, uncovered, about 3 hours.
4. Meanwhile, simmer, covered, giblets and neck with onion, carrot, and 2 cups water. Remove liver after 10 minutes; simmer rest 2 hours, or until giblets are tender.
5. Drain. Chop giblets, including liver, very finely. Discard neck and vegetables. Reserve broth.
6. Twenty minutes before end of roasting time, check turkey for doneness (thigh joint should move easily). Then pull back foil, and brush turkey with juices in foil.
7. Roast 20 minutes longer, or until nicely browned. Remove to hot platter; keep warm.
8. Make gravy: Measure juices from foil into medium saucepan; skim off fat. Add broth and water if necessary to make 3 cups liquid.
9. In small bowl, mix flour, ½ cup water, and meat-extract paste until smooth. Blend into juices; bring to boiling, stirring.
10. Add pepper and giblets. Taste; add more seasonings, if necessary.
MAKES 8 TO 10 SERVINGS

BRAZIL-NUT STUFFING

½ cup butter or margarine
2 cups chopped Brazil nuts
2 cups finely chopped celery
½ cup chopped onion
6 cups cooked long-grain white rice
1 cup seedless raisins
½ teaspoon dried rosemary leaves
2 teaspoons salt
½ teaspoon pepper

1. Melt butter in skillet. Add nuts, celery, and onion; cook, stirring, over low heat until celery and onion are tender – about 5 minutes.
2. In large bowl, with fork, toss rice with remaining ingredients and nut mixture until well combined.
3. Use to fill neck and body cavity of 10-pound ready-to-cook turkey.
MAKES ABOUT 9 CUPS STUFFING

FRESH CRANBERRY JELLY

4 cups (1 lb) fresh cranberries
2 cups water
2 cups sugar
Dash salt

1. Wash cranberries; drain, and remove stems.
2. Turn into 3½-quart saucepan. Add 2 cups water; bring to boiling point over high heat. Reduce heat; simmer, covered, 20 minutes.
3. Press cranberries and liquid through food mill or colander; then strain, to remove seeds.
4. Bring cranberry purée to boiling point; boil, uncovered, 3 minutes. Add sugar and salt; boil 2 minutes.
5. Pour into a 3-cup mold. Refrigerate for 5 hours, or until firm.
6. To unmold, carefully loosen edge of mold with a sharp knife. Turn out onto serving dish.
MAKES 8 TO 10 SERVINGS

STUFFED ACORN SQUASH

4 medium acorn squash
⅔ cup butter or margarine, melted
⅔ cup dark corn syrup
1 teaspoon salt
¾ teaspoon ground ginger
1 tablespoon grated lemon peel
1 tablespoon lemon juice
3 cans (15½-oz size) small white onions, drained
½ cup broken walnuts

1. Preheat oven to 375F.
2. Scrub squash; cut in half crosswise; scoop out seeds and stringy portion.
3. Place squash, cut side down in shallow baking pan. Add hot water to measure ½ inch.
4. Bake 45 to 50 minutes or until squash is tender when tested with fork.
5. Meanwhile, combine butter, corn syrup, salt, ginger, lemon peel and juice; mix well.
6. Turn squash; fill hollows with onions and walnuts. Spoon syrup mixture over each.
7. Bake, uncovered, 15 minutes longer.
MAKES 8 SERVINGS

BRANDIED-MINCEMEAT PIE

Pastry for 2-crust pie
1 jar (28 oz) prepared mincemeat (3 cups)
1 cup coarsely chopped walnuts
¼ cup diced candied orange peel, chopped
2 tablespoons sliced candied cherries
¼ cup brandy or sherry

1. On lightly floured surface, roll out half of pastry into an 11-inch circle. Use to line 9-inch pie plate; trim. Refrigerate, with rest of pastry, until ready to use.
2. Preheat oven to 425F.
3. In large bowl, combine rest of ingredients, mixing well. Turn into pastry-lined pie plate.
4. Roll out remaining pastry into an 11-inch circle. Make several slits near center for steam vents; adjust over filling; trim.
5. Fold edge of top crust under bottom crust; press together. Crimp edge decoratively.
6. Bake 40 to 45 minutes, or until crust is golden-brown.
7. Cool partially on wire rack; serve warm.
MAKES 6 TO 8 SERVINGS

To flame mincemeat pie:
1. Cut 4 kumquats in half, lengthwise.
2. Scoop out inside of each half.
3. Soak 8 small sugar cubes in lemon extract a few minutes; place in kumquat halves.
4. Arrange kumquat halves, on top of crust near edge of pie.
5. Take pie to table; light the sugar cubes.

A Buffet for a Crowd

Manicotti* or Lasagna*
Tossed Green Salad Bowl*
Bread Sticks   Italian Bread
Pickled Garden Relish
Custard-Filled Cream Puffs*
Red or White Jug Wine
Tea   Coffee

*Recipes given for starred dishes.

BAKED MANICOTTI
(Pictured, pages 44-45)

Tomato Sauce
1/2 cup olive or salad oil
2 cups finely chopped
  onion
2 cloves garlic, crushed
2 cans (1-lb size) tomato
  purée
2 cans (2-lb, 3-oz size)
  Italian plum tomatoes,
  undrained
1/4 cup chopped parsley
2 tablespoons sugar
1 1/2 tablespoons salt
3 teaspoons dried
  oregano leaves
2 teaspoons dried basil
  leaves
1/2 teaspoon pepper
1 teaspoon fennel seed
2 cups water

Filling
1/3 cup olive or salad oil
2 cups chopped onion

2 cloves garlic, crushed
2 1/2 lb ground chuck
2 eggs, slightly beaten
2 tablespoons salt
2 teaspoons dried
  oregano leaves
1 teaspoon dried basil
  leaves
1/2 teaspoon pepper
3 pkg (10-oz size) frozen
  chopped spinach,
  thawed, drained and
  finely chopped
1 pkg (8 oz) mozzarella
  cheese
2 pkg (8-oz size, 16 shells
  each) manicotti
2 cups grated Parmesan
  cheese
2 pkg (8-oz size)
  mozzarella
  cheese
Parsley

1. Make Tomato Sauce: In 1/2 cup hot oil in 5-quart Dutch oven or kettle, sauté 2 cups onion and 2 cloves garlic until tender – 5 minutes.
2. Add remaining sauce ingredients (mash tomatoes with a fork) and 2 cups water; bring to boil. Lower heat; simmer, covered and stirring occasionally, 1 hour.
3. Meanwhile, make Filling: In 1/3 cup hot oil in large skillet, sauté onion and garlic until tender – about 5 minutes. Turn into large bowl.
4. In same skillet, brown chuck, stirring (break up beef with wooden spoon), until well browned – about 20 minutes. Remove with slotted spoon to onion mixture; add eggs, salt, herbs, pepper, chopped spinach and 3 cups sauce; mix well.
5. Coarsely grate 1 package mozzarella; stir into meat mixture.

6. Preheat oven to 375F. In about 6 quarts rapidly boiling salted water, carefully place manicotti, a few at a time; stir gently. Boil 2 minutes just to soften; drain. With small spoon, fill manicotti with meat mixture; set aside.
7. Spoon a third of sauce into bottom of round cake pan, 16 1/2 inches in diameter, 2 inches deep; arrange, spoke fashion, half of the filled shells on top of the sauce (see Note). Cover with a third of sauce; sprinkle with half of Parmesan cheese. Place remaining manicotti on top, spoke fashion. Top with rest of sauce. Arrange slices of mozzarella on top of manicotti; sprinkle with remaining Parmesan cheese.
8. Cover tightly with foil; bake 60 minutes; remove foil; bake, uncovered, 15 minutes, or until it is bubbly. If desired, sprinkle with Parmesan and chopped parsley before serving.
SERVES 25.
Note: Two 9-by-13-by-2-inch baking pans may be used; divide sauce and filled manicotti shells between the two pans. Bake, covered, 40 minutes; uncovered, 10 minutes. Sauce and filling can be made day ahead and refrigerated. Assemble before baking.

LASAGNA FOR 25

Meatballs
2 eggs
1/2 cup milk
3 slices white bread,
  crumbled
2 lb ground chuck
1/2 cup finely chopped
  onion
2 tablespoons chopped
  parsley
1 clove garlic, crushed
1 teaspoon salt
1/2 teaspoon pepper

Sauce
1/2 cup olive or salad oil
2 lb Italian sweet
  sausages
1/2 cup finely chopped
  onion
2 cloves garlic, crushed

1/4 cup chopped parsley
2 cans (2-lb, 3-oz size)
  Italian plum tomatoes,
  undrained
4 cans (6-oz size) tomato
  paste
4 teaspoons dried
  oregano leaves
2 teaspoons dried basil
  leaves
2 tablespoons sugar
2 tablespoons salt
1/2 teaspoon pepper
1/4 teaspoon ground red
  pepper
1 cup water

1 1/2 pkg (1-lb size) lasagna
1 1/2 lb mozzarella cheese,
  diced
2 lb ricotta cheese
2 cups grated Parmesan
  cheese

1. Make Meatballs: Preheat oven to 450F. In

medium bowl, beat eggs slightly. Add milk and bread; mix well. Let stand 5 minutes.

2. Add chuck, ½ cup onion, 2 tablespoons parsley, 1 clove garlic, 1 teaspoon salt and ½ teaspoon pepper; mix until well blended. Shape into 60 meatballs – 1 tablespoon per meatball. Place in well-greased shallow baking pan.

3. Bake, uncovered, 30 minutes.

4. Meanwhile, make Sauce: In 1 tablespoon hot oil in large skillet, brown sausages on all sides, pricking with fork to release fat. Remove from skillet; set aside. In remaining hot oil in a 5-quart Dutch oven or heavy kettle, over medium heat, sauté onion and garlic until golden. Add rest of sauce ingredients, ending with pepper, and 1 cup water, mashing tomatoes with wooden spoon. Add sausages. Bring to boiling; reduce heat, simmer, covered, 1½ hours, stirring occasionally.

5. Add meatballs and drippings; simmer, covered, 20 minutes, stirring occasionally.

6. Preheat over to 350F.

7. Lightly grease a large 17-by-11½-by-2¼-inch baking pan (see Note). Cook lasagna as package label directs. Drain; rinse in hot water. Drain again.

8. Remove sausages from sauce; slice in ¼-inch pieces. In baking pan, layer half the ingredients in this order: lasagna, mozzarella, ricotta, tomato sauce with meatballs, sausage and Parmesan cheese; then repeat. If desired, additional mozzarella cubes or strips can be arranged on top before baking.

9. Bake 50 to 60 minutes, or until hot and bubbly and cheese is melted and lasagna is heated through. Let stand 20 minutes before cutting.

MAKES 25 SERVINGS

To do ahead: Cover with foil; refrigerate overnight. Next day, preheat oven to 350F. Bake 1½ hours, or until hot and bubbly.

Note: You can use 2 13-by-9-by-2-inch baking pans. Bake 35 to 40 minutes.

GREEN SALAD FOR 25

2 medium heads iceberg lettuce	1½ cups salad or olive oil
1 head (8 oz) escarole	½ teaspoon pepper
2 heads (1½-lb size) romaine	1 teaspoon dried basil leaves
1 bunch radishes	3 cloves garlic, split
	2 teaspoons salt
	1 teaspoon sugar

Oil-and-Vinegar Dressing
½ cup red-wine vinegar

1. Prepare salad greens: Wash lettuce, escarole and romaine; separate into leaves, discarding discolored or bruised leaves. Drain well, placing on paper towels to remove excess moisture. Wash and slice radishes.

2. Place cleaned greens in large plastic bag. Refrigerate until crisp and cold – several hours or overnight.

3. Make Oil-and-Vinegar Dressing: Combine all ingredients in jar with tight-fitting lid; shake vigorously.

4. Refrigerate, covered, several hours or overnight. Remove garlic before using. Makes 2 cups.

5. At serving time, tear greens into bite-size pieces into bowl; leave small leaves whole. Add radishes. Makes 12 quarts.

MAKES 25 SERVINGS

CUSTARD-FILLED CREAM PUFFS

Custard Filling	Cream Puffs
2 pkg (3¼-oz size) vanilla pudding-and-pie filling mix	1 cup water
3 cups milk	½ cup butter or margarine
1 cup heavy cream	¼ teaspoon salt
¼ cup confectioners' sugar	1 cup sifted all-purpose flour
1 teaspoon vanilla extract	4 large eggs
	Confectioners' sugar

1. Make Custard Filling: Prepare pudding as package label directs, using the 2 packages and 3 cups milk.

2. Pour into medium bowl; place waxed paper directly on the surface. Refrigerate until chilled – at least 2 hours.

3. In small bowl, combine heavy cream, ¼ cup confectioners' sugar and the vanilla; with portable electric mixer, beat at medium speed just until stiff. Fold whipped-cream mixture into pudding until combined. Refrigerate to chill well – for several hours or overnight. Makes enough filling for 24 cream puffs.

4. Make Cream Puffs: Preheat oven to 400F. In medium-size, heavy saucepan, combine 1 cup water with the butter and salt. Over medium heat, bring to boiling; remove from heat.

5. With wooden spoon, beat in flour all at once. Over low heat, beat just until mixture leaves side of pan and forms a ball – 1 to 2 minutes. Remove from heat.

6. With portable electric mixer, beat in eggs, one at a time, beating hard after each addition until mixture is smooth.

7. Continue beating until dough is shiny and satiny – about 1 minute.

(continued on page 44)

8. Drop by generous tablespoonfuls, 2 inches apart, onto ungreased cookie sheet.

9. Bake 40 to 45 minutes, or until puffed and golden-brown. Puffs should sound hollow when lightly tapped with fingertip.

10. Remove puffs from cookie sheet to wire rack. Cool completely, away from drafts.

11. To serve: With sharp knife, cut off tops of cream puffs. With fork, gently remove any soft dough from inside.

12. Fill each puff with 2 tablespoons custard; replace tops. Sprinkle with confectioners' sugar. Serve the cream puffs as soon as possible after filling.

MAKES 12 PUFFS

Note: Make another batch of cream puff dough for 24.

If you're cooking for large numbers of people, you should choose a main dish that's economical, that's easy to assemble and serve and that everybody likes. This manicotti casserole fills the bill. Manicotti shells are stuffed with a meat mixture, baked in sauce in an oversize baker's tin (recipe on page 42).

A House-to-House Dinner Party

Bouchées Mexicaines, *at far left,* are patty shells with a delicious chili-beef filling, and *above them* is chile con queso, a chile-and-cheese dip served with raw vegetables. The pièce de résistance, *at right,* is a whole Brie cheese baked in a decorated pastry crust. If you are entertaining in the winter, before sending your guests back into the cold, serve them a bowl of steaming winter-squash soup with a dollop of whipped cream. Recipes on pages 48-49.

Cocktail Surprises
Share the work and triple the pleasure with a progressive dinner party – the kind that starts at one house for cocktails, moves on to a second for the main course and to a third for dessert. If you are the first hostess, you might serve some of these delicacies along with the drinks.

1
The Menu
(Planned for 8 to 12)

At the first house, with cocktails:
Bouchées Mexicaines*
or Warm Brie en Croûte*
or Chile con Queso with
Raw Vegetables*
Butternut-Squash Soup*

Original Entrées
By the time your guests arrive for the main course, they're going to be hungry. Your entrée not only should be interesting and attractive – it should be ready. You can surely find the perfect choice from among these three – all inexpensive, and all requiring almost no last-minute attention.

2
At the second house:
Paella, Portuguese Style,*
or Cassoulet*
or Chicken Enchiladas*
or Breast of Chicken in Madeira Sauce*
Cauliflower Salad Bowl*
Tossed Green Salad Bowl
Toasted French Bread
Beer
Red or White Wine

Delicious Desserts
The dessert hostess may want to spoil her guests by offering every one of these desserts, but the display will be lavish enough if you offer only two, along with coffee and liqueurs. There are two chocolate desserts – the rich mousse and the chocolate bombe, made with ladyfingers and laced with rum. The meringue torte is a light, fluffy concoction topped off with strawberries and pineapple.

3
At the third house:
Chocolate Mousse Dessert*
or Chocolate Bombe* or
Meringue Torte*
Coffee
Liqueurs

*Recipes given for starred dishes.

BOUCHÉES MEXICAINES
(Pictured, page 46)

Filling
1 tablespoon salad oil
½ cup chopped onion
1 lb ground chuck
4 tablespoons chili powder
1 can (1 lb) tomatoes
½ teaspoon salt
½ cup red wine

2 pkg (10-oz size) frozen patty shells
1 cup grated Monterey Jack cheese

1. Make Filling: In hot oil in medium skillet, sauté chopped onion until golden – about 5 minutes. Add chuck and chili powder; cook, stirring occasionally, until browned – about 10 minutes.
2. Stir in tomatoes and salt; bring to boiling; reduce heat and simmer, stirring occasionally, 30 minutes.
3. Add wine; simmer 15 minutes; set aside.
4. Preheat oven to 450F.
5. To make pastry cases: With kitchen shears or sharp knife, cut 2-inch round from center of each patty shell. With fingers, roll remaining circles of dough into tight spirals to form 2-inch rounds.
6. Place rounds and spirals on cookie sheet covered with brown paper. Bake 20 minutes, or until golden. Remove from cookie sheet to wire rack to cool completely.
7. Scoop out soft middle of each pastry and discard. Set aside.
8. Ten minutes before serving, preheat oven to 450F; fill pastries with a heaping tablespoon of filling. Arrange on cookie sheets; sprinkle each with grated cheese.
9. Reheat in oven 5 minutes, or until filling and pastry are hot and cheese is melted. Serve hot.
MAKES 24
Note: You may prepare filling and pastries early in the morning; refrigerate filling. Proceed as in step 8.

BRIE EN CROÛTE
(Pictured, page 47)

2 pkg (11-oz size) piecrust mix
5-lb Brie cheese**
2 egg yolks
2 tablespoons water

1. Early in the day, prepare each package of piecrust mix, one at a time, as package label directs. Shape each into a ball; wrap in waxed paper. Refrigerate if not using at once.
2. On lightly floured pastry cloth, roll out one ball of pastry to an 18-inch circle. Place on large cookie sheet.
3. Remove paper from Brie, but leave outer coating intact. Place cheese in center of pastry. Bring pastry up over cheese, about 1 inch over edge. Press to make smooth all around.
4. In small bowl, combine egg yolks with 2 table-

spoons water. Beat with fork until combined. Brush a little over pastry rim on top of cheese.

5. Roll three-fourths of second ball of pastry to form a 14-inch circle; trim evenly to make 13 inches. Place on top of Brie, overlapping pastry edge; press with fingers to make a tight seal.

6. Roll rest of pastry 1/8 inch thick. With small leaf cutter, cut out 20 or more leaves, each about 2 1/2 by 1 1/2 inches. Arrange leaves around edge of pastry and in center. Brush lightly with some of egg-yolk mixture. Refrigerate.

7. About 2 hours before serving, preheat oven to 400F. Bake 20 minutes; brush again with egg-yolk mixture. Bake 20 to 25 minutes longer, or until golden-brown.

8. Remove to wire rack; let cool about 45 minutes. Remove to serving tray; serve while still warm; cut into thin wedges.

MAKES 40 SERVINGS

Note: Any leftover Brie can be refrigerated and re-heated for serving again. Bake at 350F for 20 minutes.

* * Or use a 2-pound Brie or Camembert cheese, 1 package piecrust mix and 1 egg yolk. Follow directions above, rolling three-fourths of pastry to 14-inch circle. Roll rest of pastry to 9-inch circle for top; roll trimmings for leaves. Brush with egg-yolk mixture as directed above. Refrigerate at least 1 hour. Preheat oven to 425F. Bake 10 minutes; brush again; bake 10 minutes longer. Cool 15 minutes before serving.

MAKES 16 SERVINGS

CHILE CON QUESO WITH RAW VEGETBALES
(Pictured, page 46)

1/4 cup butter or margarine	1 1/2 to 2 cans (4-oz size) green chiles (see Note), drained and chopped
1/2 cup finely chopped onion	
1 can (1 lb) tomatoes, undrained	1/2 teaspoon salt
	1 lb Monterey Jack cheese, cubed
	1/2 cup heavy cream

1. In hot butter in medium skillet, sauté onion until tender. Add tomatoes, chiles and salt, mashing tomatoes with fork. Simmer, stirring occasionally, 15 minutes.

2. Add cheese cubes, stirring until cheese is melted. Stir in cream. Cook, stirring constantly, 2 minutes.

3. Remove from heat, and let stand 15 minutes. Serve warm, in a casserole over a candle warmer, as a dip with carrot sticks, celery hearts, cucumber sticks and large corn chips.

MAKES 10 TO 12 SERVINGS.

Note: Use larger amount of green chiles, if you like this really hot.

BUTTERNUT-SQUASH SOUP
(Pictured, page 46)

4 pkg (12-oz size) frozen winter squash	1/2 teaspoon salt
	1/8 teaspoon pepper
3 cans (10 3/4-oz size) condensed chicken broth, undiluted	2 cups heavy cream
	Ground nutmeg

1. In 4-quart saucepan, combine frozen squash and chicken broth. Heat, stirring, until squash is thawed. Add salt and pepper. Refrigerate.

2. At serving time, heat squash mixture just to boiling. Gradually stir in 1 1/2 cups cream; cook slowly until heated through. Taste for seasoning; add more salt and pepper if necessary.

3. Meanwhile, beat remaining cream just until stiff.

4. Serve soup very hot. Garnish each serving with a spoonful of whipped cream; sprinkle with nutmeg.

MAKES 10 TO 12 SERVINGS

PAELLA, PORTUGUESE STYLE
(Pictured, page 51)

2 (2-lb size) broiler-fryers, each cut into 8 pieces	2 medium fresh tomatoes, peeled and chopped
1/2 cup olive or salad oil	1 bay leaf
1 lb lean pork, cut into 1-inch cubes	3 cans (10 3/4-oz size) condensed chicken broth, undiluted
2 cups chopped onion	
2 cloves garlic, crushed	1 1/2 lb large shrimp, shelled and deveined
1/4 teaspoon pepper	
1 teaspoon dried oregano leaves	1 pkg (10 oz) frozen peas, thawed
2 teaspoons salt	1/2 jar (4-oz size) pimientos
2 cups long-grain white rice	
1/2 teaspoon saffron	2 lemons, each cut into 8 wedges
1 lb Italian sausage, cut in half crosswise	

1. Wipe chicken with damp paper towels.

2. In hot oil in large skillet (10-inch), brown chicken, about 5 pieces at a time, until golden-brown all over. Remove chicken as it browns.

3. Add pork cubes to skillet; brown well on all sides. Remove.

4. To drippings in skillet, add onion, garlic, pepper and oregano; sauté, stirring, until onion is golden – about 5 minutes.

5. Add salt, rice and saffron; cook, stirring, until rice is lightly browned – about 10 minutes.

(continued on page 52)

The Portuguese-style paella *at upper right* features shrimp, chicken and sausage bedded in highly seasoned rice. The French cassoulet *(below right)* is a delicious concoction of chicken, sausage and beans. And *at lower left,* a Mexican specialty—chicken enchiladas in a red chili sauce. Serve buffet style with hot crusty bread and the cauliflower salad shown *at left* (recipes on pages 49 and 52-53).

6. Meanwhile, in another skillet, brown sausage well, turning on all sides – about 10 minutes. Drain and discard fat.

7. Meanwhile, place chicken, sausage and pork in large roasting pan, about 17 by 11 inches. Preheat oven to 375F.

8. Add tomatoes, bay leaf and chicken broth to rice mixture; bring to boiling. Add shrimp; spoon the mixture evenly over chicken and sausage in pan.

9. Bake, covered with foil (tuck foil tightly around), 1 hour.

10. If mixture seems dry, add ½ cup water. Sprinkle peas over top, without stirring. Bake, covered, 20 minutes longer, or until chicken and pork are tender and peas are cooked.

11. To serve: Turn paella into heated round serving platter or paella pan. Garnish with pimiento slices and lemon wedges.

MAKES 10 SERVINGS

CASSOULET
(Pictured, page 51)

1½ lb Great Northern white beans	1 teaspoon dried marjoram leaves
5 cups water	1 teaspoon dried sage leaves
2 cans (10¾-oz size) condensed chicken broth, undiluted	¼ lb bacon (in one piece)
2 bay leaves	½ lb salami (in one piece)
5 carrots, pared	½ lb pepperoni (in one piece)
6 onions, peeled	4-lb roasting chicken, cut in 8 pieces
4 whole cloves	2 tablespoons butter or margarine
½ cup coarsely chopped celery leaves	⅛ teaspoon pepper
1½ teaspoons salt	1 can (1 lb) peeled tomatoes
3 black peppercorns	2 tablespoons chopped parsley
3 cloves garlic, peeled and sliced	
1½ teaspoons dried thyme leaves	

1. In an 8-quart kettle, combine beans with 5 cups water; let soak about 2 hours – no longer (they will burst easily in cooking).

2. Add chicken broth, bay leaves, 2 carrots cut into chunks, 5 onions, 1 onion studded with whole cloves, celery leaves, 1 teaspoon salt, the peppercorns, garlic, thyme, marjoram and sage. Bring just to boiling; reduce heat and simmer, covered, 1 hour. Add remaining carrots; cook, covered, 15 minutes longer.

3. Meanwhile, cut bacon into 1-inch cubes. Sauté bacon until crisp, turning on all sides. Drain off fat. In medium saucepan, combine salami and pepperoni; add enough water to cover. Bring to boiling; reduce heat; simmer 5 minutes; drain.

4. Preheat oven to 350F.

5. Turn bean mixture into a 6-quart casserole. Add bacon, salami and pepperoni. Bake, uncovered, 30 minutes.

6. Meanwhile, in large skillet, brown chicken in hot butter, turning to brown well – 20 to 25 minutes. Sprinkle with ½ teaspoon salt and the pepper. Add chicken and undrained tomatoes to beans.

7. Cover top with foil; bake 30 minutes, or until chicken is tender. Bake, uncovered, 15 minutes longer. Sprinkle with parsley.

MAKES 8 SERVINGS

Note: Cassoulet is even better made the day before and reheated at 300F, covered, 1 hour before serving. If necessary, add 1 cup chicken broth or water to make it moister.

CHICKEN ENCHILADAS WITH RED CHILI SAUCE
(Pictured, page 50)

Red Chili Sauce, below	1 teaspoon salt
	¼ teaspoon pepper
Filling	
2 tablespoons salad oil	Salad Oil
½ cup chopped onion	2 cans (11-oz size) tortillas or 2 pkg (12-oz size) frozen tortillas (you'll need 24)
1 can (4 oz) green chiles, finely chopped	
2 cloves garlic, crushed	
2 cans (1-lb size) tomato purée	1 cup light cream
	2 chicken-bouillon cubes
3 cups chopped cooked chicken	1 lb Cheddar cheese, grated

1. Make Red Chili Sauce.

2. Make Filling: In 2 tablespoons hot oil in large skillet, sauté onion until tender – about 5 minutes. Add green chiles, garlic, tomato purée, chicken, salt and pepper; simmer, uncovered, 10 minutes.

3. Preheat oven to 350F. Lightly grease 2 (2-quart size) shallow baking dishes.

4. Heat ¾ inch salad oil in small skillet until very hot. Use 2 dozen tortillas. Fry, one at a time, 15 seconds on each side. Do not let them become crisp. Drain on paper towels. Set aside.

5. In small saucepan, heat cream with bouillon cubes until cubes are dissolved.

6. Dip each tortilla in cream mixture. Top each with heaping tablespoonful of filling; roll up. Place seam side down in prepared baking dishes, dividing evenly. Pour 2 cups Red Chili Sauce over tortillas in each dish; sprinkle each with half of cheese.

7. Bake, uncovered, 15 minutes, or until cheese is melted and tortillas are heated through.

MAKES 12 SERVINGS

RED CHILI SAUCE

¼ cup shortening	¼ teaspoon dried oregano leaves
⅓ to ½ cup chili powder (see Note)	¼ teaspoon cumin
¼ cup all-purpose flour	4 cups water
1½ teaspoons salt	1 can (8¼ oz) kidney beans, drained
1 teaspoon garlic salt	

1. Melt shortening in medium skillet. Add chili powder, flour, salt, garlic salt, oregano and cumin; stir until well blended. Gradually stir in 4 cups water.
2. Bring to boiling, stirring constantly; reduce heat; simmer, uncovered, 10 minutes. Add kidney beans; heat 5 minutes. Set aside.
Note: Use smaller amount if you like sauce milder, not hot. We prefer the larger amount.

CAULIFLOWER SALAD BOWL
(Pictured, page 50)

4 cups thinly sliced raw cauliflower	3 tablespoons lemon juice
1 cup very coarsely chopped pitted ripe olives	3 tablespoons wine vinegar
²/₃ cup coarsely chopped green pepper	2 teaspoons salt
½ cup coarsely chopped pimiento	½ teaspoon sugar
½ cup chopped onion	¼ teaspoon pepper
	Crisp salad greens

Dressing
½ cup salad or olive oil

1. In medium bowl, combine cauliflower, olives, green pepper, pimiento and onion.
2. Make Dressing: In small bowl, combine salad oil, lemon juice, vinegar, salt, sugar and pepper; beat with rotary beater until well blended. Pour over cauliflower mixture.
3. Refrigerate, covered, until well chilled – 4 hours or overnight.
4. To serve: Spoon salad into bowl lined with salad greens; toss just before serving.
MAKES 8 TO 10 SERVINGS

BREAST OF CHICKEN IN MADEIRA SAUCE

1½ cups long-grain white rice	Dash pepper
Salt	1½ cups dry Madeira wine
4 whole chicken breasts (about 3 lb)	1 teaspoon cornstarch
¼ cup butter or margarine	1 cup light cream
2 shallots, sliced	½ cup heavy cream
½ lb fresh mushrooms, cut in half lengthwise	1 cup grated natural Swiss cheese
1 teaspoon dried thyme leaves	2 tablespoons chopped parsley

1. Cook rice with ½ teaspoon salt and 3⅓ cups water as package label directs.
2. Wipe chicken breasts with damp paper towels. Cut breasts in half; with sharp knife, carefully remove skin and bone, keeping chicken breast intact.
3. In hot butter in large skillet, cook shallots several

minutes. Add chicken breasts; brown well over medium heat about 10 minutes on each side.
4. Add mushrooms, thyme, 1½ teaspoons salt and the pepper; cook about 3 minutes.
5. Preheat oven to 375F.
6. Turn rice into a lightly buttered, 2-quart shallow casserole. Arrange chicken breasts, overlapping slightly, down center of casserole. Arrange mushroom mixture around chicken.
7. In same skillet, pour wine into drippings; stir to dissolve browned bits in pan.
8. Meanwhile, dissolve cornstarch in 2 tablespoons light cream.
9. Add heavy cream, rest of light cream and cornstarch mixture to wine mixture; bring just to boiling, stirring. Remove from heat; add cheese.
10. Spoon half of sauce over chicken; bake in oven 10 to 12 minutes to brown slightly. Sprinkle with parsley. Reheat rest of sauce; serve along with casserole.
MAKES 8 SERVINGS

MERINGUE TORTE

6 egg whites	¼ cup light rum
¼ teaspoon salt	1 cup heavy cream, whipped
½ teaspoon cream of tartar	Whole strawberries (fresh or frozen)
1½ cups sugar	Canned pineapple slices, drained
1 teaspoon vanilla extract	

1. Day before serving or early in morning: In large bowl of electric mixer, let egg whites warm to room temperature – 1 hour. Lightly butter bottom, not side, of a 9-inch tube pan.
2. Preheat oven to 450F.
3. To egg whites, add salt and cream of tartar; beat until frothy. At high speed, beat in sugar, 2 tablespoons at a time, beating well after each addition. Add vanilla; beat until stiff peaks form when beaters are slowly raised. Turn into tube pan, spreading evenly.
4. Place on middle rack of oven. Immediately turn off heat. Let stand in oven several hours or overnight.
5. Loosen edge with spatula. Turn out torte on serving plate. Sprinkle surface with rum. Refrigerate until well chilled – at least 4 hours.
6. To serve: Frost top and side with whipped cream. Decorate top with sliced strawberries; garnish with fruit.
MAKES 10 SERVINGS

CHOCOLATE BOMBE

1 pkg (3 oz) ladyfingers
⅓ cup amber rum

Chocolate Filling
8 (1-oz size) squares
 unsweetened
 chocolate or 1½ pkg
 (6-oz size) semisweet
 chocolate pieces
1 cup butter or
 margarine, softened
2 cups unsifted
 confectioners' sugar

8 egg yolks
2 teaspoons vanilla
 extract

Chocolate Glaze
½ cup semisweet
 chocolate pieces
1 tablespoon butter or
 margarine

Candied violets

1. Line a 1½-quart bowl with plastic wrap.
2. Brush cut sides of ladyfingers with rum.
3. Arrange 6 halves of ladyfingers, cut side up, in bottom of bowl; line side of bowl in same way. Reserve rest of ladyfingers.
4. **Make Chocolate Filling:** In top of double boiler, over hot, not boiling, water, melt chocolate. Remove from hot water.
5. In large bowl, combine butter, sugar and egg yolks. With portable electric mixer at high speed, beat mixture until smooth and fluffy.
6. At low speed, gradually beat in melted chocolate and vanilla, until well blended. Turn mixture into bowl lined with ladyfingers, spreading it smooth on top. Arrange remaining ladyfingers, cut side down, over top.
7. Refrigerate 4 hours or overnight.
8. At least 1 hour before serving: Loosen side of bowl with spatula; invert on serving platter and peel off plastic wrap.
9. **Make Chocolate Glaze:** In top of double boiler, over hot, not boiling water, combine chocolate pieces and butter, stirring just until melted. Spread evenly over ladyfingers, covering completely to make a smooth glaze.
10. Refrigerate until firm – ½ hour or until serving time. To serve: Brush surface lightly with corn syrup, if desired. Decorate with a few candied violets. Serve cut in small wedges.
MAKES 20 SERVINGS

CHOCOLATE-MOUSSE DESSERT

Chocolate Chiffon Cake,
 below

Chocolate Mousse
3 cups heavy cream
1½ cups sifted
 confectioners' sugar
¾ cup unsweetened
 cocoa

2 teaspoons vanilla
 extract
¼ teaspoon salt
1 teaspoon unflavored
 gelatine
2 tablespoons cold water

1. Make and cool cake as directed.
2. **Make Chocolate Mousse:** Pour cream into large bowl; refrigerate until very cold – about 30 minutes.
3. Add sugar, cocoa, vanilla and salt; beat until stiff enough to hold its shape. Refrigerate.
4. Sprinkle gelatine over 2 tablespoons cold water to soften. Heat over hot water, stirring until dissolved. Cool.
5. Prepare cake for filling: Cut 1-inch slice crosswise from top of cake; set aside. With sharp knife, outline a cavity in cake, being careful to leave 1-inch-thick walls around center hole and side. With spoon, carefully remove cake from this area, being sure to leave 1-inch-thick base. Reserve 1¼ cups crumbled cake.
6. Measure 2½ cups chocolate cream into small bowl; fold in cooled gelatine. Use to fill cavity in cake. Replace top.
7. Mix ½ cup chocolate cream with reserved crumbled cake. Use to fill center hole of cake.
8. Frost top and side of cake with remaining chocolate cream. Refrigerate until well chilled.
MAKES 12 SERVINGS

CHOCOLATE CHIFFON CAKE

1 cup egg whites (7 or 8)
½ cup sifted
 unsweetened cocoa
¾ cup boiling water
1¾ cups sifted cake flour
1¾ cups sugar
1½ teaspoons baking
 soda

1 teaspoon salt
½ cup salad oil
7 egg yolks
2 teaspoons vanilla
 extract
½ teaspoon cream of
 tartar

1. In large bowl of electric mixer, let egg whites warm to room temperature – about 1 hour.
2. Preheat oven to 325F.
3. Place cocoa in small bowl; add boiling water, stirring until smooth. Let mixture cool about 20 minutes.
4. Into a second large bowl, sift flour with sugar, soda and salt. Make a well in center; pour in salad oil, egg yolks, vanilla and cooled cocoa. With spoon or electric mixer, beat just until smooth.
5. Sprinkle cream of tartar over egg whites. With mixer at high speed, beat until very stiff peaks form when beater is slowly raised. Do not underbeat.
6. Pour batter over egg whites; with rubber scraper or wire whisk, gently fold into egg whites just until blended. Turn batter into ungreased 10-inch tube pan.
7. Bake 65 to 70 minutes, or until cake tester inserted in center comes out clean.
8. Invert pan over neck of bottle; let cake cool completely – about 1½ hours. With spatula, carefully loosen cake from pan; remove.
MAKES 10-INCH TUBE CAKE

Beautiful Brunches

For women who love to have company but have a hectic family schedule during the week, brunch can be the answer: a relaxed, informal way to entertain. It can be served indoors or out, be a sit-down affair or a casual buffet. And without making it overly elaborate, you can treat your guests to something much more special than what they would normally have at home.

Chilled Honeydew Soup*
Golden Puffy Omelet*
Sautéed Canadian Bacon*
Warm Croissants
Blueberry Coffeecake*
Butter   Strawberry Jam
Coffee   Chilled White Wine
SERVES 6

*Recipes given for starred dishes.

CHILLED HONEYDEW SOUP

1 (4-lb) ripe honeydew melon	1/3 cup sugar
1 cup dry sherry	1 1/2 tablespoons lime juice

1. Day before: Cut melon in half; scoop out seeds. Scoop out honeydew melon meat.
2. In blender or food processor, combine honeydew melon and rest of ingredients. Blend until smooth – several times, if necessary. Refrigerate, covered, until very cold – overnight, preferably.
MAKES 6 CUPS, 8 SERVINGS

GOLDEN PUFFY OMELET
(Pictured, page 56)

10 eggs, separated	1 cup sour cream
4 slices bacon, cut into small pieces	2 teaspoons snipped fresh chives
2 tablespoons butter or margarine, melted	8 to 10 slices bread, crusts removed and halved diagonally
1 teaspoon salt	
1/4 teaspoon cream of tartar	3/4 cup coarsely grated Swiss or Cheddar cheese
Dash pepper	

1. Separate eggs; turn whites into large bowl of electric mixer, and let stand at room temperature about 1 hour. Turn yolks into a small bowl. Sauté bacon until crisp. Drain on paper towels.
2. Preheat oven to 350F. Turn butter into shallow, oval baking dish. about 13 inches long, 2 inches deep; about 3-quart volume.
3. Add 1/2 teaspoon salt and the cream of tartar to egg whites. With mixer at high speed, beat whites just until stiff moist peaks form when beater is slowly

raised. With the same beater, beat the egg yolks with 1/2 teaspoon salt and the pepper until they are very thick and lemon-colored.
4. Using a rubber spatula, gently fold sour cream, chives and bacon into yolks, to blend well.
5. With wire whisk, gently fold yolk mixture into whites until combined. Turn into prepared dish. Insert bread slices into mixture around edge of pan. Sprinkle top with the grated cheese. Bake 15 to 20 minutes, or until omelet is golden-brown and puffy. Serve at once.
MAKES 6 SERVINGS

SAUTÉED CANADIAN BACON

2 tablespoons butter or margarine	1/2 cup white wine, cider or apple juice
1 1/2 lb Canadian bacon, sliced 1/4-inch thick	

1. In hot butter in large skillet, sauté bacon gently (half at a time, in a single layer) 2 to 3 minutes on each side, to brown slightly. Remove as browned.
2. Return slices to skillet; pour wine over all. Simmer gently, covered, until heated through – about 5 minutes.
MAKES 8 SERVINGS

BLUEBERRY COFFEECAKE

2 cups sifted all-purpose flour	1 1/2 cups sugar
2 teaspoons baking powder	2 eggs
1/2 teaspoon salt	1/2 cup milk
1/2 cup butter or margarine	2 cups blueberries
	2 tablespoons sugar

1. Preheat oven to 350F. Grease well a 9-inch round layer-cake pan.
2. Sift flour with baking powder and salt; set aside.
3. In large bowl, with portable electric mixer or wooden spoon, cream butter with 1 1/2 cups sugar until light and fluffy. Add eggs, one at a time, beating after each addition until they are well blended.
4. Add flour mixture alternately with milk, beating by hand just until combined.
5. Turn into prepared pan. Gently sprinkle berries over top; then sprinkle with sugar. Bake 55 minutes, or until top springs back when gently pressed with fingertip. Let cool in pan 5 to 10 minutes before serving in wedges. Serve warm.
MAKES 10 SERVINGS

Clockwise from lower left:
Golden Puffy Omelet,
recipe on page 55.
Eggs Florentine Hollandaise,
recipe on page 62.
Scrambled Eggs Deluxe en
Croûte, recipe on page 61.

White-Wine Spritzers*
Spinach Soufflé Roulade with
Mushroom Filling*
Baked Tomato Halves*
Toasted English Muffins
Streusel Coffeecake Squares*
Butter
Apricot and Strawberry Preserves
Coffee   Chilled White Wine
SERVES 8

*Recipes given for starred dishes.

WHITE-WINE SPRITZERS

Ice cubes
1 bottle (1 liter) dry white
  wine, chilled

1 bottle (12 oz) club soda,
  chilled
8 lemon wedges

Over ice cubes in chilled 6-ounce glasses, pour half white wine, then half soda; stir. Garnish with wedges of lemon.
MAKES 8 SERVINGS

SPINACH SOUFFLÉ ROULADE WITH MUSHROOM FILLING

Spinach Soufflé
7 eggs, separated
Butter or margarine
1 pkg (10 oz) frozen
  chopped spinach
6 tablespoons all-
  purpose flour
Dash ground red pepper
3/4 teaspoon salt
1 cup milk
Grated Parmesan
  cheese
1/2 cup coarsely grated
  sharp Cheddar cheese
1/4 teaspoon cream of
  tartar

Mushroom Filling
1/3 cup butter or
  margarine
1/2 lb fresh mushrooms,
  sliced
1/4 cup unsifted all-
  purpose flour
1/2 teaspoon salt
Dash ground red pepper
1 1/2 cups half-and-half
2 egg yolks
1/4 cup dry sherry

1. Make Spinach Soufflé: Place egg whites and yolks in separate bowls. Let whites warm to room temperature – 1 hour. Grease well bottom and sides of a 15-by-10 1/2-by-1-inch jelly-roll pan; line bottom with waxed paper; then grease well with butter.
2. Cook spinach according to package directions; drain well; chop finely. Makes 1 cup.
3. Preheat oven to 350F. Melt 1/3 cup butter in small saucepan; remove from heat. With wire whisk, stir in 6 tablespoons flour, red pepper and 1/2 teaspoon salt until smooth. Gradually stir in milk.
4. Bring to boiling, stirring constantly. Reduce heat. Simmer, stirring, until mixture is thick and leaves pan. Beat in 1/4 cup Parmesan, the Cheddar and chopped spinach.
5. With whisk, beat yolks; beat in cheese mixture. With mixer at high speed, beat whites with 1/4 teaspoon salt and the cream of tartar until stiff peaks form when beater is slowly raised.
6. With an under-and-over motion, fold one-third of the whites into cheese mixture. Carefully fold in remaining whites to combine.
7. Turn into prepared pan. Bake 15 to 20 minutes, or until surface is puffed and firm when pressed with fingertip.
8. Meanwhile, make Mushroom Filling: Melt butter in medium saucepan. Add mushrooms; sauté, stirring occasionally, about 5 minutes. Remove from heat; stir in flour, salt and pepper until smooth.
9. Add half-and-half; cook over medium heat, stirring constantly, until mixture comes to boiling; boil 1 minute. Remove from heat.
10. In medium bowl, beat egg yolks well. Stir in 1/2 cup hot sauce; return egg-yolk mixture to hot sauce in saucepan. Add sherry.
11. Cook over low heat, stirring, until heated through. Do not boil.
12. With metal spatula, loosen edges of soufflé. Invert on waxed paper sprinkled with 2 tablespoons Parmesan. Peel off waxed paper.
13. Spread surface evenly with 1 cup filling. From short side, roll up; place, seam side down, on warm, greased, heatproof serving platter. If desired, garnish with sautéed mushroom slices. Pass remaining sauce.
MAKES 8 SERVINGS

BAKED TOMATO HALVES

4 large tomatoes (about
  1 lb)
1/2 cup butter or
  margarine
1/2 cup finely chopped
  onion
2 teaspoons prepared
  mustard

1 teaspoon
  Worcestershire sauce
4 slices white bread, torn
  into coarse crumbs
1 tablespoon chopped
  parsley

1. Preheat oven to 350F. Wash tomatoes, and remove stems. Cut in half crosswise. Place, cut side up, in shallow baking pan.
2. In half of hot butter in medium skillet, sauté onion until tender. Stir in the mustard and Worcestershire. Spread on tomato halves.
3. Melt remaining butter in same skillet. Stir in the bread crumbs and parsley. Sprinkle over tomatoes.
4. Bake, uncovered, 20 minutes, or until the tomatoes are heated through and crumbs are golden-brown.
MAKES 8 SERVINGS

**Fresh Orange Spritzer; Scrambled Eggs,
Sunday Style; Sautéed Canadian Bacon
(recipes on pages 55 and 60).**

STREUSEL COFFEECAKE SQUARES

Streusel Mixture
½ cup light-brown sugar, packed
2 tablespoons butter or margarine, softened
2 tablespoons all-purpose flour
1 teaspoon ground cinnamon
½ cup coarsely chopped walnuts (optional)

Batter
1½ cups sifted all-purpose flour
2½ teaspoons baking powder
½ teaspoon salt
1 egg
¾ cup granulated sugar
⅓ cup butter or margarine, melted
½ cup milk
1 teaspoon vanilla extract

1. Preheat oven to 375F. Grease an 8-by-8-by-2-inch baking pan.
2. Make Streusel Mixture: In small bowl, combine brown sugar, 2 tablespoons soft butter, 2 tablespoons flour, the cinnamon and nuts; mix with fork until crumbly; set aside.
3. Make Batter: Sift flour with baking powder and salt; set aside.
4. In medium bowl, with rotary beater, beat egg until frothy. Beat in granulated sugar and butter until well combined. Add milk and vanilla. With wooden spoon, stir in flour mixture until well combined.
5. Turn half of batter into prepared pan. Sprinkle evenly with half of Streusel Mixture. Repeat with remaining batter and streusel mixture.
6. Bake 25 to 30 minutes, or until cake tester inserted in center comes out clean. Cool slightly in pan on wire rack. Cut into squares. Serve warm.
MAKES 9 SERVINGS

Fresh Orange Spritzer*
Scrambled Eggs, Sunday Style*
(in Brioche)
Sautéed Canadian Bacon,* page 55
Toasted English Muffins
Assorted Preserves
Coffee
SERVES 4

*Recipes given for starred dishes.

FRESH ORANGE SPRITZER
(Pictured, page 59)

2 cans (6-oz size) frozen orange juice concentrate
1 cup cold water
1 bottle (1 pt, 12 oz) club soda, chilled

3 tablespoons lemon juice
Ice cubes

1. In a large pitcher, combine the orange-juice concentrate and 1 cup cold water; stir until the orange juice is thawed.
2. Add soda, lemon juice and 2 cups ice cubes.
MAKES 6 TALL SERVINGS

SCRAMBLED EGGS, SUNDAY STYLE
(in Brioche)
(Pictured, page 59)

4 individual brioches (from bakery)

Scrambled Eggs
7 eggs
¼ cup milk
½ teaspoon salt
Dash pepper

2 tablespoons butter or margarine
1 pkg (3 oz) chive cream cheese, cut in ½-inch cubes

Chopped parsley or chives

1. Preheat oven to 350F. Heat brioches on cookie sheet.
2. Meanwhile, make Scrambled Eggs: In medium bowl, combine eggs, milk, salt and pepper; with rotary beater, beat just until combined.
3. Heat butter in a large skillet. Pour in egg mixture; cook over low heat. As eggs start to set on bottom, gently lift cooked portion with spatula to form flakes, letting uncooked portion flow to bottom of pan.
4. Add cheese; cook until eggs are moist and shiny but no longer runny.
5. Cut off tops of brioches; set aside. With fork, scoop soft inside from center of each brioche.
6. Spoon eggs into brioches; sprinkle with parsley; replace tops.
MAKES 4 SERVINGS

Bloody Marys or Piñas Coladas*
Scrambled Eggs Deluxe en Croûte*
Bacon Curls   Grilled Ham
Warm Pecan-Coffeecake Ring
Oranges Brûlot*
Coffee or Caffè Espresso
SERVES 8

*Recipes given for starred dishes.

PIÑAS COLADAS

½ cup cream of coconut (see Note)
1 cup unsweetened pineapple juice, chilled

⅔ cup light rum
2 cups crushed ice

1. Refrigerate six cocktail glasses, to chill well — about 1 hour.
2. In electric blender, combine cream of coconut, pineapple juice, rum and ice; cover, and blend at high speed ½ minute.

3. Pour into chilled glasses. If desired, serve with a pineapple spear.

MAKES 1 QUART; 8 SERVINGS

Note: Cream of coconut may be purchased as coconut-milk cream.

SCRAMBLED EGGS DELUXE EN CROÛTE
(Pictured, page 57)

18 eggs	2 tablespoons chopped
¾ cup milk	fresh chives
1¼ teaspoons salt	Braided Loaf, below
Dash pepper	¼ cup butter or
2 tablespoons butter or	margarine, melted
margarine	
3 pkg (3-oz size) chive	
cream cheese, cut into	
½-inch cubes	

1. Make scrambled eggs: In medium bowl, combine eggs, milk, salt and pepper; with rotary beater, beat just until combined.
2. Heat 2 tablespoons butter in a large skillet. Pour in egg mixture; cook over low heat. As eggs start to set on bottom, gently lift cooked portion with spatula to form flakes, letting uncooked portion flow to bottom of pan.
3. Add cheese and chives; cook until eggs are moist and shiny but no longer runny.
4. Split Braided Loaf in half lengthwise. With fork, scoop some of the soft inside from center. Brush inside of loaf with melted butter.
5. Spoon eggs into hot bread, and serve.

MAKES 10 SERVINGS

BRAIDED LOAF (see Note)

1½ cups milk	2 pkg active dry yeast
¼ cup sugar	3 eggs
1 tablespoon salt	6½ cups unsifted all-
½ cup butter or	purpose flour
margarine	2 tablespoons water
½ cup warm water	
(105-115F)	

1. In small saucepan, heat milk just until bubbles start to form around edge of pan. Remove from heat. Add sugar, salt and butter, stirring until butter is melted. Cool to lukewarm.
2. If possible, check temperature of warm water with thermometer. Sprinkle yeast over water in large bowl of electric mixer, stirring until dissolved. Stir in milk mixture.
3. Add 2 eggs and 3 cups flour; beat with electric mixer until smooth – about 2 minutes. Gradually add 3 more cups flour, mixing in with hand until dough is stiff enough to leave side of bowl.
4. Turn out dough onto pastry cloth or board floured

with remaining ½ cup flour. Knead until smooth and elastic – about 10 minutes.
5. Place in lightly greased large bowl; turn dough over to bring up greased side. Cover with towel; let rise in warm place (85F), free from drafts, about 1½ hours, or until double in bulk.
6. Turn out dough onto lightly floured pastry cloth or board. Divide into quarters. Using palms of hands, roll three of the quarters into 26-inch-long strips. Braid; press ends together to seal. Place braid on greased large cookie sheet. Mix remaining egg with 2 tablespoons water; use some to brush top of braid; reserve rest. Divide remaining quarter of dough into three pieces. Roll into 26-inch-long strips, and braid. Place directly on top of first braid; press ends together to seal.
7. Let rise in warm place, free from drafts, until double in bulk – 50 to 60 minutes.
8. Place oven rack in middle of oven. Preheat oven to 375F.
9. Brush surface with remaining egg mixture.
10. Bake 30 to 35 minutes, or until a rich golden-brown. (If crust seems too brown after 25 minutes of baking, cover with foil or brown paper.) Remove to wire rack to cool. Serve warm, as directed in Scrambled Eggs Deluxe en Croûte.

MAKES 1 LARGE BRAID

Note: If desired, you may purchase a large braided loaf, about 18 inches long and 6 inches wide. Heat, wrapped in foil, and use as directed above.

ORANGES BRÛLOT
(from Antoine's, New Orleans)

8 medium-size navel	8 oz brandy (1 cup)
oranges	Mint sprigs
8 small sugar cubes (or	
halved regular cubes)	

1. Place oranges in a large kettle; cover with boiling water; let stand 5 minutes.
2. With slotted utensil, lift out one orange at a time. While orange is still warm, cut skin (not fruit) around center of the orange. To form cups at top and bottom, carefully fold back skin. Do not remove skin.
3. To serve, stand the orange on one cup on a dessert plate. Place a sugar cube in top cup. Slowly heat brandy (a small amount at a time) in small saucepan or brandy warmer. Pour warm brandy over sugar in cup; ignite.
4. When flames subside, brandy is sipped with spoon, then orange is eaten.

MAKES 8 SERVINGS

Chilled Papaya Filled
with Sliced Strawberries
Eggs Florentine Hollandaise*
Sautéed Ham Slices
Basket of Assorted Hot Rolls
Butter
Sour-Cream Coffeecake*
Coffee
Chilled Champagne or White Wine
SERVES 8

*Recipes given for starred dishes.

EGGS FLORENTINE HOLLANDAISE
(Pictured, page 56-57)

1 pkg (10 oz) frozen patty shells	1 cup half-and-half
½ pkg (11-oz size) piecrust mix	1 teaspoon salt
	⅛ teaspoon white pepper
Creamed Spinach	⅛ teaspoon ground nutmeg
3 pkg (10-oz size) frozen chopped spinach	½ cup grated Swiss or Gruyère cheese
3 tablespoons butter or margarine	
¼ cup finely chopped onion	8 eggs
3 tablespoons all-purpose flour	Hollandaise Sauce, below

1. Preheat oven to 450F. Bake patty shells as package label directs. Remove and discard soft inside and soft part underneath center cap.
2. Prepare piecrust mix as package directs for one-crust pie. Shape into a ball. Reduce the oven temperature to 400F.
3. On lightly floured surface, roll pastry into a 12-inch circle; trim edges.
4. Fold pastry in half; transfer to an 11-inch tart pan. Unfold pastry; fit into bottom of tart pan. Prick entire surface evenly with fork.
5. Bake 15 to 20 minutes, or until golden-brown. Remove to rack.
6. Prepare Creamed Spinach: Cook spinach as label directs. Drain very well, pressing out excess liquid in colander; drain on paper towels. In hot butter in saucepan, sauté onion over medium heat 5 minutes.
7. Remove from heat. Stir in flour. Gradually stir in half-and-half. Bring to boiling, stirring. Add drained spinach, salt, white pepper, nutmeg and grated cheese; cook 3 minutes, stirring. Keep warm.

8. Poach eggs: In shallow pan or skillet, bring water (about 1 inch deep) to boiling point. Reduce heat to simmer. Break each egg into a saucer; quickly slip egg into water. Cook, covered, 3 to 5 minutes. Lift out of water with slotted pancake turner or spoon. Drain well on paper towels.
9. Make Hollandaise Sauce.
10. To serve: Gently remove outer rim from pastry, keeping shell on bottom. Cut patty shells in half down through top. Arrange, cut side down, around pastry to make a rim. Fill pastry shell with Creamed Spinach. Arrange poached eggs on top. Spoon Hollandaise Sauce over each egg.
MAKES 8 SERVINGS

HOLLANDAISE SAUCE

2 egg yolks	¼ teaspoon salt
¼ cup butter or margarine, melted	Dash ground red pepper
1½ tablespoons lemon juice	

1. In top of double boiler, using wire whisk or fork, slightly beat egg yolks.
2. Slowly stir in butter, beating constantly.
3. Cook stirring, over hot water (water in double-boiler base should not touch bottom of pan above) just until thickened.
4. Remove double-boiler top from hot water. Gradually beat lemon juice, salt and pepper into sauce.
5. Cover and keep hot over warm water until serving.
MAKES ABOUT ⅔ CUP

SOUR-CREAM COFFEECAKE

2 cups sifted all-purpose flour	¾ cup sour cream
1 teaspoon baking powder	
½ teaspoon baking soda	**Crumb Topping**
¼ teaspoon salt	½ cup granulated sugar
½ cup butter or margarine, softened	¼ cup sifted all-purpose flour
1 cup granulated sugar	2 tablespoons butter or margarine, softened
3 eggs	1 teaspoon ground cinnamon
1 teaspoon vanilla extract	
	Confectioners' sugar

1. Preheat oven to 350F. Grease well and flour a 9-inch tube pan.
2. Sift 2 cups flour with the baking powder, soda and salt; set aside.
3. In large bowl of electric mixer, at high speed, beat ½ cup butter, 1 cup granulated sugar, the eggs and vanilla, occasionally scraping bowl with rubber scraper, until light and fluffy – about 5 minutes.
4. At low speed, beat in flour mixture (in fourths) alternately with sour cream (in thirds), beginning and ending with flour mixture. Beat just until smooth – about 1 minute.
5. Turn batter into prepared tube pan.
6. Bake 50 minutes, or until cake tester inserted in center comes out clean.
7. Meanwhile, make Crumb Topping: In small bowl, combine all topping ingredients; toss lightly with fork until mixture is crumbly.
8. Remove cake from oven; sprinkle Crumb Topping evenly over top. Return to oven 10 minutes.
9. Let cool in pan on wire rack 10 minutes. Remove from pan; sprinkle crumb-topped surface with confectioners' sugar. Serve warm.
MAKES 10 SERVINGS

Sea Breezes*
or Sliced Strawberries in
Fresh Orange Juice
Finnan Haddie Delmonico*
Hot Scones*
Butter   Currant Jelly
Assorted Danish Pastries
Coffee
SERVES 8

*Recipes given for starred dishes.

SEA BREEZES

1 cup vodka (see Note)	¾ cup cranberry juice
2 cups unsweetened grapefruit juice	Ice cubes

1. Day before: Combine vodka, grapefruit juice and cranberry juice in blender; blend to mix well.
2. Refrigerate, covered, several hours or overnight, to chill well.
3. To serve: Blend again, or stir to mix well. Pour over ice cubes in tall glasses.
MAKES 8 SERVINGS
Note: Vodka may be omitted, if desired.

FINNAN HADDIE DELMONICO

2-lb piece smoked haddock	Dash ground red pepper
¼ cup butter or margarine	1 cup milk
3 tablespoons all-purpose flour	1 cup half-and-half
½ teaspoon salt	5 hard-cooked eggs
	4 thin slices buttered toast, cut diagonally in half

1. Rinse fish in cold water. If large, cut in half. Place in medium skillet. Add water to cover; bring to boiling; reduce heat; simmer, covered, 15 minutes.
2. Drain well. With a fork, separate fish into flakes. (You should have 2½ cups.) Set aside.
3. Melt butter in medium saucepan. Remove from heat; blend in flour, salt and pepper. Gradually stir in milk and half-and-half.
4. Bring to boiling over medium heat, stirring. Reduce heat; simmer 5 minutes, stirring occasionally.
5. Peel eggs; slice three. Chop whites of remaining two eggs, and put yolks through sieve. Cut toast into triangles.
6. Add fish and sliced egg to sauce; simmer 1 minute.
7. Turn into heated shallow serving dish. Sprinkle with chopped egg white and sieved yolk. Arrange toast triangles around edge. Serve immediately.
MAKES 8 SERVINGS

HOT SCONES

3 cups packaged prepared biscuit mix	2 tablespoons butter or margarine, melted
¼ cup sugar	1 egg white, slightly beaten
2 whole eggs	
1 cup mashed potato	

1. Preheat oven to 400F. Lightly grease baking sheet.
2. In large mixing bowl, combine biscuit mix, sugar, whole eggs and mashed potato; using fork, mix until smooth – dough will be soft.
3. Turn out dough onto lightly floured pastry cloth. Knead five times.
4. Roll dough to ¼-inch thickness. Cut into 2½-inch squares. Brush with melted butter; fold over to make a triangle, pressing edges lightly to seal.
5. Place on prepared baking sheet, 2 inches apart. Brush with egg white.
6. Bake 8 to 10 minutes, or until golden-brown. Serve warm with butter.
MAKES 1½ DOZEN

Chilled White Wine
Eggs Tetrazzini With Spinach Twists*
Whole Wheat Italian Bread
Sliced Oranges and Honeydew
With Cointreau*
Caffè Expresso with Lemon Twist
SERVES 6

*Recipes given for starred dishes.

EGGS TETRAZZINI WITH SPINACH TWISTS

6 eggs	2 cups milk
Salt	1 cup grated Swiss
1 pkg (16 oz) spinach	cheese
twists (pasta)	1 cup grated sharp
1/4 lb medium	Cheddar cheese
mushrooms	1/4 cup grated Parmesan
1/4 cup butter or	cheese
margarine	Dash pepper
3 tablespoons all-	
purpose flour	

1. Place eggs in a medium saucepan; cover with water to 1 inch above them; bring rapidly to boiling. Take pan off heat; cover, and let stand 20 minutes.
2. Bring 3 quarts salted water to boiling in a large saucepan. Add spinach twists. Boil, uncovered and stirring occasionally, 8 to 12 minutes. Drain very well; return to a dry saucepan.
3. Meanwhile, wash and slice mushrooms. Melt 1 tablespoon of the butter in a medium skillet. Add mushrooms: sauté, stirring occasionally, until golden. Add to drained pasta, and toss until well combined. Cover and keep warm.
4. Meanwhile, combine flour and 1/4 cup milk in a medium saucepan. Stir with wire whisk until smooth. Gradually beat in remaining milk. Bring to boiling over medium heat, stirring constantly, until thickened.
5. Add Swiss cheese, Cheddar cheese, 2 tablespoons Parmesan cheese, 1/4 teaspoon salt and the pepper; cook over low heat, stirring constantly, until sauce is blended and fairly smooth. Keep warm.
6. Place eggs in cold water until they are cool enough to handle. Then peel and rinse them; slice eggs in half lengthwise.
7. Turn pasta into serving dish. Arrange eggs on top. Pour sauce over all. Sprinkle with remaining Parmesan cheese. Serve immediately.
MAKES 6 SERVINGS

SLICED ORANGES AND HONEYDEW WITH COINTREAU

3 large navel oranges, chilled	1/2 cup Cointreau or other orange liqueur
1/2 large honeydew melon, chilled	

1. Peel oranges; slice crosswise. Peel honeydew; slice into 1/8-inch-thick crosswise slices. Cut orange slices into 2-inch pieces.
2. In a large chilled bowl, layer oranges and melon. Pour Cointreau over all. Refrigerate until serving.
MAKES 6 SERVINGS

Chilled Grapefruit Juice
Pecan-Oatmeal Pancakes*
Crisp Bacon
Coffee
SERVES 4

*Recipes given for starred dishes.

PECAN-OATMEAL PANCAKES

1 1/2 cups uncooked old-fashioned oats	1/4 teaspoon salt
1 cup unsifted all-purpose flour	1 1/2 cups milk
1/2 cup coarsely chopped pecans	2 eggs
2 tablespoons light-brown sugar	2 tablespoons butter or margarine, melted
2 teaspoons baking powder	Salad oil

1. In a medium bowl, combine oats, flour, pecans, brown sugar, baking powder and salt.
2. Combine milk, eggs and butter in a small bowl or 2-cup measuring cup. Beat with fork or wire whisk until well combined.
3. Pour the egg mixture over the dry ingredients. Stir just until they are combined.
4. Meanwhile, slowly heat griddle or heavy skillet. To test temperature, drop a little water onto hot griddle; water should roll off in drops.
5. Lightly oil griddle. Spoon on about 1/4 cup batter for each pancake. Cook until bubbles form on surface and edges become dry. Turn; cook about 2 minutes longer, or until underside is golden-brown. Serve immediately with butter and warm maple syrup.
MAKES 16 (4-INCH) PANCAKES